Misadventures in Motherhood

FIONA LOONEY writes a regular column in the *Sunday Tribune*.
She has also worked for *Hot Press*, for BBC Radio in London and as a
scriptwriter for RTÉ, and is a regular on the 'Gerry Ryan Show'. She
lives in Dublin with her husband, Steve, and their three children.

Misadventures in Motherhood

Life with **The Small Girl**, **The Boy** and **The Toddler**

FIONA LOONEY

THE O'BRIEN PRESS

DUBLIN

First published 2005 by The O'Brien Press Ltd,
20 Victoria Road, Dublin 6, Ireland.
Tel: +353 1 4923333; Fax: +353 1 4922777
E-mail: books@obrien.ie
Website: www.obrien.ie

ISBN: 0-86278-929-X

This book is based on columns originally published in the *Sunday Tribune*.
'Power of Dreams' pages 198-200 was first published in *Woman's Way*.

British Library Cataloguing-in-Publication Data
A catalogue record for this title is available from the British Library

1 2 3 4 5 6
05 06 07 08 09

Editing, typesetting, layout and design: The O'Brien Press Ltd
Printing: Cox & Wyman Ltd.

Cover design: Sin É Design

Photo credits: Author photograph on page 2 courtesy of the *Sunday Tribune*

To Ciara, Cian and Uainín,

with love and apologies.

FIRST BORN

AGE: 2 WEEKS (1997)

For the past two weeks, I have been living without dignity. I have not worn make-up or perfume, I have scarcely looked in a mirror, and when I have, it has been only to marvel at the collection of pimples that has erupted on my too-old chin. My fingernails, once seriously long and perfectly polished, are cut to the quick and clinically clean. I walk around in *flip flops*. Last week, I left my hair, previously washed at least once every twenty-four hours, a whole five days without even the rub of a flannel. I have had tubes and needles cavorting in my veins, and my every orifice has been designated a shrine to the medical profession. For a week, I wore elastic support stockings.

I have discussed my waterworks with complete strangers, and I've invited them to examine the evidence. I've *asked* for suppositories and appreciated their stinging relief. Details of my bowel movements have been shouted across the rooftops of North London, and all day every day, I smell very slightly of stale milk. Congratulate me. I have had a baby.

There were complications, and then some. Without reproducing the contents of what became a fantastically impressive medical file, suffice to say that if the pregnancy was unplanned, then the birth came as a complete bombshell.

I believed I had reached an understanding with the unborn child that it would make an appearance on the last day of July, as scheduled – preferably about 1.30pm, because I would be having my lunch then and could squeeze it in, or out, as the case may be.

Unfortunately, The Baby had neither social graces nor any concept of deadlines, and contrived with my ailing body to make it in time for Ladies' Day at Royal Ascot. She arrived *sans* hat, but rest assured that, eight weeks early and smaller than I want to think about, she was very quickly assigned one.

It's amazing how the human mind works. The two things that people tell you when you've just produced a minuscule morsel are that their sister/friend/mother/neighbour had a baby that was a pound and is now six foot seven, and – more cryptically – that you have a nice tan. The amateur psychologists had a field day. I have now heard details of some fifty babies born with neither hope nor body fat, who went on to become gigantic builders, accountants and Olympic champions. Curiously, none of the one-pound-wonders seems to have ended up being, say, five foot seven and working in a stationer's, but perhaps I'm just being shielded from those examples by concerned friends and relatives.

The bit about the nice tan was more difficult to analyse, particularly as it came almost without exception from medical experts, and was usually preceded by phrases like 'blood pressure off the chart, body draining itself of protein, looking very grim – but hey! Nice tan.' There is an old and poor joke that ends with the line 'the daffodils are out early,' and for a week, with my ailing body and my glorious tan, I was that joke. The bronzed look is now gone, since I had neither the opportunity nor the inclination to moisturise it. In the end, it came away in big chunks that gave me the appearance of Michael Gambon in 'The Singing Detective', and put a halt to the nice tan brigade, who began instead to say things like 'nice nightie', but with less conviction in their voices.

Meanwhile, all the unpleasantries went the way of the tan and I am left with an uninviting scar and a small but perfectly formed daughter. She is, inevitably, recovering from all this much better than I am. Indeed, when the intensive care nurse announced that she had passed 'a soft yellow stool', I was briefly jealous.

She is also, lest I gave the wrong impression earlier, considerably more than a pound, so please don't write to me with more examples of Pound People. Details of tiny girls who succeed in life despite being lumbered with their fathers' enormous noses will probably serve her better in the long term in any case.

In the meantime, emotionally wrought and psychologically all over the place, I have spoken to a counsellor. Actually, I have spoken *at* a counsellor, which is quite a different thing. Counsellors are not normally people that I would consort with, but this one happened to be in the right place at the right time (though this may not be her interpretation of the incident), and unfortunately for her, was wearing a hospital ID badge with the word *Counsellor* writ large on it. She also asked me how I felt, which to my mind was a mistake. If you take one lesson from all this to your own life, let it be never to ask a woman who's just given birth eight weeks early how she feels. Trust me, your life is too short for the answer. Certainly, and probably for fear she would miss her own children growing up, my counsellor was almost crying with relief when I stopped. 'Still,' she said cheerfully, 'At least you can verbalise it. Nice tan.'

I had another counselling session on the day I left the hospital, this time from a midwife who wanted to talk to me about contraception. She showed me a diagram, and I nodded sagely, resisting every urge to string the words 'stable', 'horse' and 'bolted' together into a meaningful sentence.

Then my mother phoned to warn me not to get pregnant that night, which is more or less what she did, and only goes to show that she is a hardier individual than her daughter. That said, I hobbled down to the chemist the very next day and kitted myself out with the all-new, all-natural, all-miraculous Persona. Though, with the way my wretched body is feeling at the moment, and like the good Catholic Irish girl I am, 'twas more in fear than in hope.

SMALL GIRLS' CLUB

AGE: 5 MONTHS

Nobody warned me before The Small Girl was born that her arrival on this Earth would propel me unwittingly into a gigantic club of similarly afflicted people who would stop in the street and talk to me without knowing the first thing about me. If I'd known in advance, I could have dusted off my phony smile.

Despite nine months of nods and winks, you're not truly in the club until you're parading your progeny the length and breadth of the world. Then, without so much as checking the small print, you discover that you've been inducted into an association of parents and small children: a harried bunch of individuals who wander the streets in search of other members and other tales of sleepless nights and luckless nappies. It is as though we are all on a quest to find a worse child than ours: a smaller, sadder, fatter, balder small person to give us some hope that our own is not so bad after all. Deep down, we fear that the other man's grass is greener and so we must scour the streets for scorched earth.

Meanwhile, in pursuit of a life less ordinary, we travel to Westport. But the club is everywhere. In the hotel bar, toddlers wobble over to check out The Small Girl and are quickly followed by stooping parents (anthropological note: the only time in his life that adult man does not walk fully erect is when his children are toddling). They come to retrieve their charges and are suddenly radiant to stumble across fellow card-carrying members of the club.

We talk, according to the club articles, through the children, in those extraordinarily high voices reserved for talking to other people's children yet – curiously – not our own. In best 'Jackanory' intonation, I ask one child her name and in an identical voice, her mother tells me it's Aoife. Still looking at the child, I indicate that this may well be the most exciting news I've ever heard, while the other woman asks The Small Girl how old she is and I tell Aoife she's nearly five months.

And so it continues, until we've exchanged sleeping, eating and general carrying-on habits of both children without ever addressing each other. Aoife and The Small Girl and the hundreds of other Aoifes and Small Girls out there, meanwhile, watch their parents bond in this most nonsensical way and vow never to behave in such an embarrassing manner when they grow up.

Of course, if it weren't for the children, we'd never talk to each other at all. Without their scampering sorties into other members' camps, we'd simply tramp through the Neolithic remains of County Mayo by day and eat and drink by night, and nobody would ever quiz us on which of the Teletubbies carries the handbag.

Without our living, breathing bonding devices, we wouldn't know how much sleep the people at the other table got the previous night and whether or not you can bring a buggy on the Clare Island ferry. These are the things we need to know.

Needless to say, before all this, I'd rather have eaten my own legs than talk to strangers. Perhaps I was too well trained in the never-talk-to-strangers department as a nipper, but I really don't find any entertainment in talking to people I've never met before. God knows I'm not shy, but I tend to think that if common interests haven't thrown us together by now, it's unlikely that there were any common interests to begin with.

It is like the story told about the legendary Jim Hand, who used to decline introductions to strangers on the basis that 'I know enough people already.' He once, according to popular folklore, told Bono that he would like to be his friend, but that the U2 star would have to wait until one of Jim's existing friends died, as there were no vacancies at the moment. Like Big Jim, I too know enough people. But now, all of a sudden, I know even more.

The positive side of all this outreaching is that once The Small Girl goes to school, I won't have to talk to anyone again until I'm really old. After all, we only feel compelled to talk to strangers when we are in the club and again, briefly, before we die.

You'll already have noticed this, of course. People in their twilight years simply can't keep themselves to themselves, conversing with strangers at every turn, every bus stop and in every shop. It is as though, having spent years saying nothing to nobody, they suddenly realise they have a hell of a lot to say and very little time left in which to say it all.

Although club members only talk to each other, elderly people talk to everyone and expect no conversation in return, especially if they are in full flight with another old person, when it is simply two monologues happening in close proximity, the two orators happy simply to have found each other.

It goes without saying that when a club member meets an old person, chaos ensues. Old women are sure of most things, but above all that whatever you are doing to your child, you are Doing It Wrong. Hence you get nice old ladies on trains complaining about your breast-feeding position and insisting that your child has wind. One woman passed me in the street – PASSED me, mind – and then shouted back that The Small Girl needed fruit juice.

When you dare tell them you have a fundamental belief in

sterilising bottles, they laugh ruefully and tell you that unsterilised bottles never did anyone any harm and people today have gone mad altogether. At which point you look wildly around in the desperate hope that a club member will come to your rescue with a high-pitched tale of how their baby was sick for a week after eating something he found under the lino. Luckily, like a particularly frazzled guardian angel, there's always one around when you need one.

THE COST OF LOVING

AGE: 14 MONTHS

With slightly open mouth I read a newspaper article about kids demanding school uniforms designed by Versace and Tommy Hilfiger and I wonder at the poor, harassed parents who spend a fortune caving in to these hideous children. With jaw firmly on the floor, I then listen to the sullen shoe-shop assistant who assures me that if I spend less than £30 on The Small Girl's first proper shoes, then I may as well bind her feet and have done with it. Not for the first time, it occurs to me that a cocaine habit would probably have been considerably cheaper to cultivate than a miniature human being.

I suppose we should consider ourselves lucky that The Small Girl hasn't yet started to fleece us in any real and knowing way, but in the brief time left to us before she discovers the nuances of big business, there are plenty of other so-and-sos around to fill the void and empty our wallets. None has thus far proved more efficient in this department than the shoe world. There is a whole page in my souvenir baby book devoted to the first shoes business, which suggests that it is supposed to be one of those special, bonding moments that the video camera should be drafted in to capture for posterity. With this in mind, it is presumably a terrible thing to actually begrudge your own child their first shoes, but there you have it. I cannot believe that it is really necessary to spend thirty quid on something that, sullen girl assures me, will last about six weeks. You don't need Leaving Cert maths to work that out as a fiver a week for shoes that go nowhere and spend most of their short life being carried by their laces from one room to another over the shoulder of The Small Girl. And by the time she needs a school uniform Philip Treacy may well be designing berets. Every time I turn on my radio the Manic Street Preachers caution me that if I tolerate this, then my children will be next. It occurs to me that if I tolerate this, then my children will actually be well dressed and I will be bankrupt. It is a bad business.

Those of you with older children already know this, of course, and it won't have escaped your attention that the television ad campaigns for the Christmas toy market now kick off in earnest sometime around September. Between the hours of six and seven in the morning – peak viewing time for youngsters – the toymakers run riot around the commercial breaks in the sure knowledge that the parents who are up are not sufficiently on the ball at that hour to 'Just Say No'. And what delights await the little girls of the western world this Christmas morning! My personal favourite is the toy beauty salon and wedding chapel combined, where the blushing bride can be made up and styled before repairing to the chapel to marry Mr Right and get a lovely wedding ring for her trouble. What makes this toy particularly magical is that the bride in question is actually a horse. While I'm all in favour of feeding children's imaginations, by suggesting to little girls that one day they might grow up to marry a horse, I fear we may be nurturing a future generation of mini Caligulas with nuclear capability. The

Husband loves that ad as well because it contains an unfortunate line about the newly wed horse showing everyone her ring, which at half six in the morning seems like the funniest thing he's ever heard.

Even the more conventional dolls these days must have some sort of spin. Barbie, a poor girl's Sindy when I was a nipper but now queen of all she surveys, has somehow spawned a number of younger sisters since I last looked, and all without losing her fabulous figure. One of Barbie's sisters is black, but I'm far more interested in the youngest one, who is called either Poppy or Stacy (all dolls these days are called either Poppy or Stacy) and who comes complete with a baby's bottle and her very own car. On the same shelf as Hula Barbie, Rapunzel Barbie, Ski-ing Barbie, Ballet Barbie and all the other many dimensions of this wonder woman, I can only assume that young Poppy/Stacey is a sort of Child Prodigy Barbie, that she will do a degree in applied mathematics at Oxford University before she is seven and have a nervous breakdown and a conviction for possessing drugs by the time she hits puberty, at which point she may well reinvent herself as Jailbird Barbie.

Thankfully, The Small Girl is still too daft to enter the magical world of Barbie and her talented sisters and have her head turned by horses of the marrying kind. Indeed, on her last visit to Massive Toy Warehouse In the Middle Of Nowhere, she ran past millions of magical moments retailing at £39.99 and selected instead a small ball that cost her grateful mother 50p. But I fear this frugal approach to the business of growing up won't last. As soon as she begins taking note of ads for baby dolls with full driving licences, I shall start taping the Open University and playing it over the commercial breaks. If they do a course on how to make your own shoes, all the better.

HELLISH BABYSITTER

AGE: 20 MONTHS

Somehow, we would appear to have fallen into the clutches of the most promiscuous babysitter in North London. If her smile as she shows us off our own premises gets any wider, I fear we will have to start charging her.

It is not the physicality of her time in our home that I resent as much as the fact that we are paying for it. While we spend good money to sit with strangers in airless restaurants in the desperate hope of mixing up a little magic, The Babysitter is languishing on our sofa with Mr Tonight, performing acts of prestidigitation that would turn the heads of the entire Fossett family. I know this because a) I have an extremely vivid imagination, b) I used to be seventeen and c) I have seen the evidence with my own eyes. Actually, I have only seen what was left of the evidence, but even the all-trusting husband agreed that a piece of cellophane that shape could only have come from a cigarette or a condom packet, and since we can both smell people smoking in the flat second next door to ours, we could only come to one terrible conclusion: on our night of nights, The Babysitter had got considerably further than we had.

While the finding of the cellophane might easily have been the cue for a burst of outrage followed closely by an irate phone call containing a standard you'll-never-work-in-this-town-again clause, I am quite proud to report that it caused barely a ripple of concern in the living room of shame. For a brief moment, I was quite impressed that The Babysitter was practising safe sex, even if I

wished she was doing it somewhere else. These feelings, however, were quickly replaced by an irrational mixture of envy,
horror and admiration – fuelled by memories of many teenage
years of babysitting, one boyfriend and a handful of desperate tus-
sles on a sofa, punctuated by my urgent warnings of imminent
returns and his bewildered protests about only wanting to put his
arm around me. Of course in those days in Ireland, a condom
wrapper on any floor was grounds enough for imprisonment, but
frankly the only evidence the good people who paid my wages
were ever likely to find was my utter mortification that I had a boyfriend in the first place.

To the promiscuous babysitter's credit – and indeed following
my own example from many years ago – she always tells us in
advance about her gentlemen callers; but while I had company for
only a tiny number of my long dark nights, the promiscuous
babysitter is racking them up for every single visit these days. We
have even met one – a young man who didn't utter a single word
while we were there and whose only grand gesture towards his
genial – if largely absent – hosts was to drive the promiscuous
babysitter home, thus saving us the cab fare. For all that, it was
something of a false economy, since we stayed out much later
than we'd intended in order not to embarrass ourselves upon our
return by interrupting some more important business than our
own. When we did finally get home, we even took the precaution
of coughing loudly outside the door, but the promiscuous babysitter is nothing if not professional, and all was as it should have
been.

For all that, most people think we're mad. My friend around the
corner, who has no babysitter, was so horrified at the cellophane
incident that she threw away the phone number of the promiscuous babysitter's friend who also babysits, and more or less vowed

never to go out again. Since the friend's name was Jade and the number a mobile, there seemed to be a good chance that she was moonlighting as a prostitute, and in that case, I can't say I blame my friend – though equally, I don't envy her social life.

Besides which, we are half fascinated by the life we have afforded the promiscuous babysitter and wholly reluctant to find another in a place where half the childminders seem to be psychotic and the other half unavailable. Our girl may lead a fantastic life, but she is honest and reliable and, since The Small Girl is a small wonder when it comes to going to bed and staying there, we have never had to worry about her rudely interrupting proceedings in the room below her. And if it wasn't for that pesky piece of cellophane on the floor, I could even fondly believe that the men of the moments are as luckless as my own suitor way back before video recorders revolutionised the babysitting world.

But all is about to change. The promiscuous babysitter is off to see the world (as if she hasn't seen quite enough from our sofa) and The Husband has propositioned a girl in the off-licence on our behalf. She starts next week. I haven't yet had a chance to assess her promiscuity level but if she does turn out to be a creature of the night, then at least she is Irish – so she should have the good grace to feel guilty about it.

UNDERWHELMING UNDERWEAR

AGE: 22 MONTHS

The longer you are married, the more comfortable your underwear is. Just as anniversaries increase in value as the years go by, the quality of the married person's underwear diminishes so that as the diamonds and rubies of long-standing unions beckon, there is no silk left to celebrate them in. We embark on the matrimonial adventure with a heart full of romance and a drawer full of satin impracticalities and lace frivolities, and then we stand aside while soft cotton and things that don't go up your rump in the night creep in and take their place. Like rings on a tree, it is possible to measure the age of a relationship by counting how many layers of off-white knickers you have to plough through before you find something black and painful. When it gets to the stage where you only take the silly ones out so you can both have a laugh and shake your heads at the preposterousness of it all, then you know that your marriage has found its own level and it is nowhere near the bottom drawer.

This, then, is the complacency the priest warned us about at our pre-marriage course (shortly after he cautioned The Husband with some confidence that it was only a matter of time before he came home from work and discovered I'd spent all the housekeeping on a hat), but frankly, we are both too knackered and I am too pregnant to raise our game. In any case, it was having a child that did for the underwear drawer in the first place. I had no idea, before that fateful day when I exchanged my gorgeous, push-me-pull-you black Wonderbra for a nice, white, look-ma-no-wires maternity number, that a bra could actually be comfortable. I almost wept when the shop assistant said I couldn't wear it home. After that, I could never regard the miraculous Wonderbra with quite the same degree of enthusiasm again, and a little nagging piece of me suspects that the only reason we're doing it all again is so I can return to the cosy bras with impunity.

I could say the same for the knickers, only I never stopped wearing them. Maternity knickers, once I discovered them, were just too comfortable, too friendly, to ever really discard. While the satin and lace did make a brave attempt at a revival between times, they were never going to push those grand, cotton, stretchy rivals too far from the top of the drawer. And now they too are legitimately back and, secure in the knowledge that these days I really don't have an option, all's right in the world and the underwear department.

The only blot on the otherwise rosy horizon is the rather ominous mutterings of midwives concerning dates, sizes, heights of funduses and the like. Having produced one baby so small you had to know where to look just to see her, it now appears that I'm poised to make up for it by having a baby of regular weight, plus the pounds that The Small Girl lacked. Consequently, it is a long time since I've actually seen my underwear and already those Most Comfortable Knickers In The World are showing signs of strain. And so, enter the Unreliables.

So christened by The Husband because they once fell down in Tesco's and had to be abandoned in the off-licence, the Unreliables are my last resort knickers; a pair so stretched and perished that, if I ever have that road accident in them, I would rather be run over again than have the medical world sniggering into their stethoscopes at me. And yet, the Unreliables have become a sort of underwear touchstone – an insecurity blanket, if you like – that may travel right to the back and bottom of the drawer, but because of their emotional value (and, I suppose, because of the Tesco's incident) can never be discarded. And at times like these, they are God's gift itself. Already this week, on their return to active service following a long lay-off, they have fallen down while I washed the kitchen floor, and it is only a matter of time before they repeat the performance in public and strip me of that final shred of dignity that must inevitably go in any case before the labour ward beckons.

The other thing that happens to people after they settle into marriage is that they become obsessed with the price of other people's houses, and always read every word of the property supplements, until one day they find themselves inexplicably drawn to the deaths announcements instead. I did intend to devote some time to this curious business but I seem to have become caught up in the history of my underwear – from Unbelievable to Unreliable in Under Three Years – instead. When your own knickers become like stealth bombers (you may not be able to see them but by God you know they're there), it's difficult not to.

ABOUT THE BOY

SMALL GIRL: 2 YEARS
BOY: 2 WEEKS

Amidst a great deal of puking, The Small Girl has been joined by a substantial boy. In the interests of public decency, I will spare you the hilarious birth story – suffice to say that he clocked in at almost three times the birth weight of the previous tenant and, when he opened one critical eye to survey the shambles in his wake, I wasn't at all convinced that he'd been worth the effort. He will, I trust, grow into his looks.

Of course, the worst aspect of the whole sorry business was my own performance. Having been the Patient-With-The-Ready-Quip for the past nine months, I suddenly dried when the spotlight fell on my cervix (seriously, they had a spotlight) and became Patient-In-An-Unfeasible-Amount-Of-Pain-And-Unable-To-See-The-Funny-Side, a transformation that was a huge disappoint-ment to the hospital staff and all those visitors they invited in for a quick root around my nethers. Oh yes, the jokes came thick and fast the next day: 'If you were my wife, I'd want you to be con-scious,' said the evil doctor with the busy hands. 'If I was your wife, I'd definitely want to be unconscious,' came my hilarious reply, a full twenty-four hours later. 'We can put up a screen if it makes you feel more comfortable,' cooed a fidgety midwife. 'What? So you can show it outside the hospital as well?' said the patient, as she was discharged. You get the picture, and no, it's not a pretty one. It's not that the jokes weren't there; it's just that they were time delayed.

In this respect, what I regret most about the whole ordeal is that I didn't make the most of the opportunity to insult The Husband. The hours spent in the delivery room are a fantastic time of diplomatic immunity for any woman, where we can say whatever the hell we like and put it down to the drugs, the pain or the combination thereof. You will never again be able to tell your husband where to go with quite as much passion and venom as you can when you are poring forth – and you will never again have such a sterling opportunity to do so without any fear of blame or reprisal. All those things you've been meaning to say to him for years can come out in one breathless monologue – the bit about him never mowing the lawn and everything – and all he can do is smile weakly and agree that he is the worst bastard ever put on this Earth. You can even call him by the C-word, and the whole world, knowing that you are giving birth to his child, will nod in agreement and forgive you in an instant. If you can get beyond the extreme pain, the indignity, the puking and unpleasantness, it's a marvellous time.

So as you can imagine, failing to come up with a single coherent insult has left me feeling particularly wretched. Many women grieve when they give birth; most mourn for the loss of pregnancy and some grieve for the older children who must now share the spoiling. I am grieving for the lost opportunity to call my husband a bollox. More than that, I am bereft because I couldn't muster a single 'you got me into this mess ... if you ever come near me with that thing again' style barb; in fact, the midwife managed to deliver more thinly veiled threats of castration than I did. And even when they announced that the bump was a boy bump and showed me his tiny willy to prove it, I still didn't think to trumpet that he was just like his father/more man than his father or any of the million ready-made one-liners women can fall back on at times like this.

There is always the option of retrospective action, but the immunity is gone and every insult will now have its consequence. I know a woman who split up with her partner because he had the gall to wink at her in the delivery room – the bastard! – and who later regretted that she hadn't just grievously injured him at the time instead of allowing the incident to fester till her stitches came out. The problem with delaying the labour- room barrage is that by the time The Baby blows its first sicky bubble, the humour's usually gone off you and the father is restored to his rightful position as the bloke who will bring you in the wrong knickers the next day. Twenty-four hours later, the memory of the pain has begun to fade, the jokes all have punchlines and the proud father makes you laugh so much you almost burst your stitches. And then you know that there was a time to wreak vengeance on his head, but strangely and miraculously, that time is now gone forever.

HELL IN THE TROPICS –
The Lanzarote Experience

SMALL GIRL: 2 YEARS, 4 MONTHS
BOY: 10 WEEKS

The sun has got its balaclava on, so instead of heading for the beach and a panoramic view of the extraordinarily persistent cloud which appears to have paid its sunbed hire for a fortnight in advance, we stay by the pool. Swimming pools have always made me nervous because people tend to talk to each other there, and already on this holiday I've had three women of uncertain provenance come up and tell me that I'm 'very brave' for bringing a ten-week old baby to a place so far away from Boots.

As it turns out, they're not entirely wrong. Ten minutes poolside and The Boy begins to howl like he's never howled before. The Husband is muttering obscenities about a man in swimming trunks with 'Third Millennium Technology' written on them – something to do with his poor see-sawing technique and the fact that he's almost catapulted The Small Girl to the beach while his beloved Chelsea (oh, yes) stays rooted to her end of the Marjorie Daw apparatus. He's clearly in no mood to go through the meningitis checks with me at this early stage, so I return to the apartment to check how stiff the crying boy's neck is.

It isn't, but the noise is getting worse, his nose has started to run and he's refusing to open his eyes. I do all the things a good mother should do in these situations: ignore him, try to make him laugh, look at him as though I've never seen him before, and finally put on a top and go see a woman about a doctor. The hotel receptionist assures me that an English-speaking medicine man will be at our door in ten minutes and I go back to try to disguise the fact that the child has been sleeping in our suitcase.

Forty minutes later I send The Husband to enquire gently as to the elusive doctor's intentions, and the receptionist eats him alive for not answering the phone call that would have told us that the doctor can't be arsed coming out to our apartment and that we must go into town to see him. His protestations that the phone hadn't rung do little to quell the woman's outrage, and five minutes later a man with a black bag is on our doorstep to repair the phone while The Boy – who has now turned a curious shade of pink because I've been holding him too close to my non-colour-fast bikini top – screams on.

And then, as babies will, he stops. And since we, too, couldn't be arsed making a journey on a day like today, I go to the receptionist and tell her we won't be needing the doctor after all and she calls me by an obscene name even before I've left reception.

Back at the pool, the Third Millennium Technology man's wife is talking to another woman about how she sorts her holiday washing, so I start to chase The Small Girl around the playground. Now, if this amenity were in our bit of Europe, it would be made of plastic or rubber. Here, it's made of solid concrete so that when I crack my skull against the roof of a tunnel I didn't see coming, I understand for the first time in my life why people talk about reeling from blows to the head. For a couple of seconds I'm unsure whether I will pass out, vomit, or just die: my head feels as though it's been pushed down my neck and into my body. The pain is so overwhelming that when I scrape my badly sunburnt back against a thorn bush on my stagger away from the tunnel, I don't even feel it.

Then I do, and by the time the feeble sun sets I feel a hell of a lot more besides. We're too shattered to go into town so I make some corned beef hash and slice my finger open on the tin. There is a dramatic quantity of blood, and the only way I can stem the flow is by keeping my right arm raised over my head and pressing cotton wool to the wound, making it virtually impossible for me to feed The Boy before he retires to his suitcase.

In the end, The Husband holds the child to my breast and we settle back to watch *There's Something About Mary*, which he's illegally copied onto a videocassette currently showing on the tiny VDU of our camcorder. I'm so exhausted I fall asleep *during* the dog-torturing scene.

And somewhere, somehow, in the middle of all that, The Small Girl learns to swim. A truly monumentous day.

SCARY DOLLS

SMALL GIRL: 2 AND A HALF
BOY: 5 MONTHS

Whoever said that the most frightening thing in the world would be if a flower suddenly spoke to a man obviously never saw Baby First Steps. For those who don't spend most of their waking hours watching commercial breaks on children's television, Baby First Steps is a doll who – and I mean the italics quite sincerely folks – *gets up from a crawling position on the floor and walks towards you with her arms outstretched.* It is the stuff of nightmares; the kind of thing you expect to see in a late night Hammer Horror after you've over-indulged on strong cheese and your least favourite drink. Like Frankenstein's monster, it is an aberration: it goes against nature.

Of course, the little ones love it. Children today take their dolls shaking and stirring, and the more animated the model the greater the sales. So now we have dolls who talk, who walk, who burp and wee, who drink real liquid and cry real tears and who go apeshit if their soothers are removed. And for those girls who find human beings too mundane, there are ponies that sing and monkeys that cling and a hundred and one creatures great, small and battery-operated in between. I used to think the only truly scary toys in the world were Victorian dolls, but at least their haunted faces couldn't smile real smiles. My First Love or My Baby Love or My Only Love can. Be afraid, be very afraid.

It doesn't take a psychologist to figure out that all these virtual babies can't be good for a junior mother, but it's vaguely reassuring all the same to read clucking newspaper articles at this time of year from people with letters after their name begging parents only to buy dolls who do nothing. This is fine by me – though I would like to reserve the right to purchase ones whose heads fall off on St Stephen's Day, as I'm a great believer in tradition. It's also fine by The Small Girl, who's still on the stupid side of three and hence enjoys a wildly imaginative play-life in which unanimated pieces of plastic enjoy bathing, dressing, nappy changing and suppers of pretend chicken that they're not expected to sing for. Like a Danielle Steele heroine, one of these pampered babies has recently escaped from the attic that held her captive for some twenty-five years, has had her name changed from Janet to Lucy and is currently enjoying again the kind of violent attention once administered by my own fair hand. And all the time, she does nothing but look slightly concerned. I realise that all this is just a phase The Small Girl's going through and that by, oh, next week or so, she'll be screaming for a more sophisticated charge, but while it lasts, it's a joy and something of a relief to behold.

The only possible way of avoiding the whole scary doll phase is for us to try to channel The Small Girl's substantial energies into housework. It is both a source of wonder and disappointment to me that this little woman, who will live almost her whole life in the third Millennium and will see women rule the world, enjoys nothing so much as sweeping the floor, making tea and minding babies. She is behind me right now, making up a dolls' bed with clean linen while I'm sitting at a computer, furiously sending her signals about career, liberation, independence and, well, typing. And yet nothing of what I do in this corner of the room interests her. It may be my computer that puts food in her mouth, but it is my iron that makes me a sort of heroine to her.

And she is not alone. All her little friends have let down their politically correct, emancipated mothers by demanding pots and pans and Hoovers and washing machines for Christmas, when we've done everything we can to encourage them to ask for My First Briefcase, My Little Briefcase and My Only Briefcase. I used to believe that it was social conditioning that made little girls out of sugar and spice and all things nice, but we've never pointed The Small Girl in the direction of domestic service (though now that she's so keen, it would be churlish to refuse the help), and I can only conclude, sadly, that women really enjoy a life of drudgery.

Still, where there's artificial life, there's hope. The only way to redeem these hopeless little girls is to rush out a range of dolls that includes Baby Diarrhoea Attack, My Little Immunisation Reaction, and My First Rear Molar. By next Christmas they'll be begging for backpacks and round-the-world hiking holidays, to be relished until My Little Biological Clock finally lets them down all over again

NEW YEAR'S RESOLUTIONS

SMALL GIRL: 2 AND A HALF
BOY: 5 MONTHS

My New Year's resolutions are to learn to use chopsticks, pass my driving test, stop eating the children's leftovers and spend less time with my family.

The first is a matter of some urgency, and has been forced upon me by the rest of the country becoming skilful with non-pronged cutlery while I wasn't looking. Somewhere between my moving to London five years ago and last summer, everyone in Ireland has learnt how to transport noodles and rice from plate to mouth without the aid of stainless steel. I can only conclude that you've all been to a secret seminar – possibly in 1997 while childbirth had turned my head the other way – and that this is why places like Mao (which, frankly, would have been laughed at before I left for bigger smoke) are packed with bright young things filling their bellies without the aid of a safety fork. I have become the only person in Dublin restaurants who needs to ask for cutlery, and I've tired of the sympathy of non-nationals. So for 2000, chopsticks it is for me.

The second, the driving test thing, has also now gone beyond the stage of being mildly cute and endearing and has become a roaring nuisance. Being green and motor-less is all well and good when you can zip around your world on public transport with your arms swinging, but the double buggy has done for all that and now I'm in danger of becoming the Howard Hughes of the new millennium. So if I'm to make an impression on more than just my sofa this year, I need wheels and a piece of paper that says I'm entitled to drive them.

My third resolution, concerning clearing the children's plates, threatens to be the trickiest of all to execute – particularly if The Small Girl's enthusiasm for supernoodles continues to be a feature of this new year. A combination of childhood warnings about starving children in Africa and a miserly make-up have meant that I've always found it almost impossible to throw away food, but while grown-up leftovers can usually be recycled into soups, sauces and sandwiches, chicken nuggets and half-chewed fish fingers tend not to inspire even the most innovative cook. So for the sake of the starving millions, I've been polishing them off myself.

The only problem with this wizard scheme is that I recently saw a truly gargantuan woman present herself to Ricki Lake or Oprah Winfrey or some other Guardian of Girth and confess that it had all started to go (dramatically) pear-shaped for her when she'd started eating her kids' food. By the time she appeared on television she was the size of a studio and was experiencing breathing difficulties lying down in her trailer-park home (actually, she didn't mention that she lived in a trailer park, but somehow I just knew), and her kids were threatening to have her stuffed and mounted by the eldest girl's boyfriend, as is the way of these things. Although she was no longer supernoodle twistin', she put the fear of God into those of us who were only getting started. And so, though it goes against every fibre in my body, the finger-lickin' must stop.

As to my fourth and final new year's resolution, I decided to spend less time with my family a couple of weeks ago when I was on a plane without my kids for the first time in two-and-a-half years. Taking sublime pleasure in lowering your own table-top is as good an indicator as any that you need more time to yourself. And, if I'd wanted another one, it came courtesy of the RTÉ make-up woman who asked what my cleansing routine was and what moisturising cream I used, forcing me to admit that the answer to (a) was that I sometimes put a bit of baby lotion on my face and to (b), none.

Meanwhile, aside from putting The Small Girl's pyjamas on the five-month-old boy, The Husband successfully managed to keep both little people alive and reasonably content while I was away for the night, so I've decided to take him up on the offer he's yet to make to do it all again soon. In the meantime, I've started dreaming dangerous daydreams of childminders and nurseries, just so that I can begin to do things like cut my toenails again.

I realise that it's an ambitious programme of resolutions, but since I haven't made any at all since I was about fifteen, I reckon I've got some backdated will-power due to me. If it all goes according to timetable, I might even try to lose a stone by

February. Given my previous experiences with chopsticks, I suspect one will follow the other in any case.

STARTING FINISHING SCHOOL

SMALL GIRL: 2 YEARS, 8 MONTHS
BOY: 7 MONTHS

I'm thinking of putting The Small Girl's name down for that school in Switzerland Fergie has chosen for her gels. I have three good reasons for this: 1) she'll mix with a better type of class; 2) she will grow up less afraid of snow than her mother; and 3) it will annoy the hell out of all the people who, since The Boy was born, have advised me to put his little name down somewhere suitable.

In fact, you could say my sudden interest in silly Swiss schools is my contribution to the great education inequity. It is a sad fact that in her two-and-a-half years of illiteracy, nobody has lost any sleep over The Small Girl's schooling or the postcode wherein it may occur. But in the seven months since The Boy joined the party, I've been advised that Blackrock College no longer takes boarders, that somebody I know knows somebody who might be able to get him into Gonzaga and that in any case, we've already left it too late to get him in anywhere decent.

So, on behalf of women everywhere, I am taking a stand. My daughter will go to a pointless Swiss palace of education and my son will go to a hedge school. If I've to set it up myself and die for Ireland in the process, all the better.

Of course, I'll probably chicken out of the whole Swiss adventure at the last minute – quite possibly on the same day our fees cheque bounces back from Berne to College Green. For despite its obvious charms, the Swiss school is a boarding establishment (otherwise the school run would be hell) and while I'm keen to see substantially less of my children, I'm not sure I'm ready for that degree of separation.

Besides which, I'm not at all convinced that boarding schools are good for the soul. Aside from the year in which I read Enid Blyton's *Mallory Towers* books and reeled around drunk on midnight feasts and ginger beer, I never really liked school enough to stay the night. And in the years since it was an option, I've never met any former boarders who have convinced me that my initial instincts were misplaced. The only woman I know who went to boarding school insists she had a great time but tells stories of truly awful things being put in her bed on her first night there, and the handful of men between them offer a curious mixture of repression, arrogance and excessive homosexuality that I can only conclude had its roots at the educational chalkface. In addition to that, and based on the evidence of the past week, if The Small Girl were to board, I suspect I would have to go with her and I'm not sure I'd be up for all those after-dark larder raids.

I say this because we have just started playgroup and I say 'we' because it would appear that I am to be as much a pupil as she is. So far, I have spent exactly the same amount of time at playgroup as she has. I am not alone in this: two other mothers of new pupils have also failed to exit the premises – the difference is that while they actually *intended* staying each time, I am there under extreme duress. So they roll playdough and row, row, row their boats with the same enthusiasm as their offspring while I just get covered in paint that I haven't touched and check my watch every couple of minutes to see if it's possible for time to move any slower.

This is not entirely due to discomfort with the jollier side of child rearing – though I have always found the business of singing 'Incy Wincy Spider' in public while dressed in a fleece and no-name jeans a profoundly depressing experience. Rather, it has to do with the stone-and-a-half of idiot Boy attached to my person-age in a community centre when he and I should be at home spending quality time together and eyeing each other up suspi-ciously. The Small Girl, for her part, races around, draws hopeless pictures and generally has a wonderful time ignoring her mother, until I dare glance at the door, and then she goes apeshit.

The only light at the end of this tunnel of frivolity is the reassur-ance that I need to do this for just another two years before the authorities will intervene and insist I leave the building. I'm already anticipating that glorious day as the graduation I never had. On the Friday, I shall wear a cap and gown and drink cham-pagne, and then on the Monday I will put the fleece back on and begin all over again with The Boy. That is, of course, if I can get him in somewhere at such short notice.

WELCOME TO THE JUNGLE

SMALL GIRL: 2 YEARS, 10 MONTHS
BOY: 9 MONTHS

It has come to my attention that the walls surrounding all the light switches in our home are exceedingly grubby. Which is strange, because I'm not aware of missing that often. In fact, neither I nor The Husband can ever recall an incidence of trying to turn on a light and coming away disappointed, so we can only conclude that some dirtbird is breaking into our flat in the depths of the night and get-ting his jollies from almost flicking on and off all our lights.

Of course, this is the kind of thing you only ever notice when it comes time to sell your home. Until the day your humble abode goes on the market, it is, generally speaking, just home; its tattiness is part of its character and all its faults and failings fade into long-finger DIY limbo. But come the glorious day that somebody else's description of your four walls appears under a spotlight in an estate agent's window and your home suddenly becomes a property, its smallest shortcomings become giant flaws and its quirkiness a millstone round its and your neck. Grubby walls in a home are part of that lived-in look. In a property, they may well be five grand off the asking price.

If only it ended there. Five days into the whole business of selling, buying and moving house, and the cracks are already beginning to show. They began in the marriage and – perhaps more ominously – they have now travelled down to the staircase. I kid you not: as the second person to come see what the estate agent urged early viewing on tramped down the stairs, I, in her wake, witnessed a serious chunk of wall come away from the skirting board and land on the bottom step, laughing at both me and my asking price. The marriage, the earlier casualty, was dealt a blow when Viewer Number One commented that our kitchen was 'a good size' and Husband Number One contradicted her by pointing out that it is, in fact, 'a bit small'. If an artist had ever wanted to capture a glare in oils and pick up a two-bedroomed garden flat into the bargain, he would only have had to knock on our door in those precious seconds that followed.

Luckily, the status quo was quickly restored by my own basic house-selling mistakes. Our back garden, in case you're browsing, is not north facing, as I'd told both comers, but is in fact *north-westerly*. And eating a bowl of home-made and extremely potent guacamole between visitors is not, as it turns out, an ideal way of creating the correct ambience, as it just replaces the smell of clean-ing fluids with the pungent pong of garlic – neither of which, apparently, captures the character of a unique conversion that boasts many unusual gothic features (yes, we know about the brewing fresh coffee trick, but frankly, stuffing the laundry, the spare duvets, the shopping and umpteen toys into the garden shed seemed more important at the time).

And now there will be no peace till we're out of here. Every-where I look, I see chips and flaws and cracks and marks and things that go bump in the surveyor's report. The indelible biro marks on the hall wall where I – *what was I thinking of?* – marked the kids' heights every three months and wrote the date beside each little measure. The fact that the kitchen units appear to be sinking, with the crack over the washing machine yawning wider every time I move the knife block that obscures it to peep in in trepidation. The front garden with its three bags full of rot from the summer before last. That tree that I butchered in the back garden which is refusing to grow any leaves in a sort of mini-protest. The black mark on the bath that I noticed when we came to view this place almost four years ago – the first thing we were going to put to rights.

And then there is the time factor and the fact that The Small Girl and the idiot Boy are together conspiring to bring down the value of our only fixed asset. Every day brings a new stain on the living-room carpet; every mealtime finds one more bit of banana glued to the kitchen wall. Add this dramatic depreciation to the sudden subsidence, the collapsing staircase and the marriage cracked from side to side and I can only conclude that the next few months are going to be a tad tricky. 'By the time I've finished presenting this flat, you'll want to buy it yourselves,' the estate agent had promised.

By the time he's finished, we may have to.

PRETTY GIRL

SMALL GIRL: 3 YEARS
BOY: 11 MONTHS

Just when it seemed as if my social life had gone the way of the dinosaurs and Bird's Angel Delight, my friend Graham's party finds me rubbing shoulders with a range of top-drawer celebrities, telling one devastatingly handsome TV star my entire life story – with a slight edit on The Husband and children front – and getting the night bus home (alone), pleased as punch. And Luke's party ends in the kind of fight I haven't witnessed since bands used to get high on the happy side of the Trinity Ball.

Best of all, the fight at Luke's is over The Small Girl, who is Luke's girlfriend (official) but who lately has been the object of Ben's attentions to boot. Being cuckolded at your own birthday party is bad at the best of times, but when you are three and your girlfriend (official) is being hugged between your own goalposts in your own garden by your own best friend, then things are always likely to end in tears. 'My son is obsessed with your daughter,' Ben's mother explains to me apologetically. 'That's all very well, but she's promised to Luke,' retorts the mother of the birthday boy, as her son stares dolefully at his Buzz Lightyear cake. The centre of his and Ben's universe, meanwhile, skips around oblivious to the trouble she's causing until she correctly deduces that there are 'no girls' toys here' and demands to be shown her party bag and the way to go home.

We float down the road on a cloud of happiness; she in possession of a yo-yo, a plastic bracelet and a Freddo, and me, like a slightly drunk Miss Haversham, dreaming of some sort of unspecific revenge that I may now be able to wreak on bastard men through the charms of my delightful daughter.

It is a wholly unexpected and most welcome development in our little world. Somehow, and in spite of the odds spat out by a cruel combination of genetics and sheer chance, we have ended up with a pretty daughter. The Boy may be something of an eyesore, but once he gets over his bitter disappointment with his lot and cheers up a bit he will hopefully develop the kind of dynamic personality and ultimately bank balance that women are willing to overlook looks for, but the girl, admired by strangers in supermarkets, seems destined to date from the top shelf. As a bit of a bargain-basement woman myself, I couldn't be more proud. The fact that she can barely speak and is incapable of remembering anything for longer than three seconds no longer matters: my daughter is a looker, and life is so much easier for ladies with looks.

The irony of all this is that we were actually aiming for brains. I was one of those annoying children who were always several books ahead of the rest of the class, The Husband is far from stupid, and my brother-in-law is the cleverest person I've ever met. Put that in your melting pot and stir it, and we might have been forgiven for having the computer, the easel and the baby grand all ready for our prodigious offspring to pour forth upon as soon as she could hold her own. Instead, she gazes up at us with enormous brown eyes and takes three days to learn the number on our front door, and we couldn't be happier.

In fact, the only cloud on this new, sunny dawn comes in the shape of genetically modified babies, which, the newspapers have been whispering darkly, are only a pitter-patter away. The people who made the sheep have now put the Dolly mixture into a pair of lambs and they are, apparently, only gorgeous. Meanwhile, the scientists who have unlocked the genetic code – or whatever that bit of excitement was all about – aren't ruling out engineering humans to be disease-free and disaster-proof in the near future. If they are all that, they will surely be more: beautiful people from birth who will all have enormous eyes and know instinctively what to do with them.

So here we are, unexpectedly gifted with a pretty child at a time when the competition is about to get unbelievably tough. It's all very well being a looker when there is a whole variety of dogs on the pitch as well, but if everyone else is benefiting from blinding science, then your baby browns will only get you so far. At least Miss Haversham never had to worry about her Estelle being on the same dance card as some turbo-charged beauty who'll never get a headache. Plus, she didn't have to think about the future for a boy who perpetually looks as though he's chewing a wasp.

And look how mad she went! I may as well set fire to myself now, and have done with it.

AU PAIR

SMALL GIRL: 3 YEARS, 4 MONTHS
BOY: 1 YEAR, 3 MONTHS

It has long been my ambition to relate amusing accounts of an au pair's misadventures, but somehow, I'd always hoped that the au pair in question would be my own. Instead, since the new prosperity has paused on our doorstep only long enough to wave a wad of dosh and a middle finger in our direction, it is the bungling of Bahain, somebody else's foreign body, that I bring you.

Oh, it's the usual stuff: crying in the night, putting the saucers in the toaster, misunderstanding instructions with the hilarious consequence that children remain uncollected from school, and that general class of carry-on. What makes Bahain more curious than most is that she seems to have confused me with someone who gives language lessons.

It all started when our paths kept joining en route to nursery school with our respective charges. Smiles and nods quickly gave way to observations about the rain (me: 'It's raining again.' her: 'Why?'). Now, just a few short weeks later, she has taken to phoning me up at all hours to ask me what the word for carrot is – and trust me, you've no idea how surreal *that* conversation is to have over the phone – and which bus she should get to Brent Cross. All that I could deal with, because at least it wasn't transacted in full view of strangers. But this week, she asked me to teach her to sing 'Twinkle Twinkle Little Star' in the playground, in front of other people.

Now, there may be some mothers out there who positively get off on 'Twinkle Twinkle', but regretfully for the foreign au pairs of this world, I am not one of them. It is bad enough to have to sing the bastard thing a couple of hundred times a week for your own children without having to put on outdoor performances of it for the amusement of adults. But Bahain knows nothing of these nuances of Western European lifestyle: all she knows is that 'Twinkle Twinkle Little Star' is one of several million things she doesn't know, and on Monday, she wanted to put that right. Of the many profoundly humiliating experiences that parenthood has brought to my world, this had to be top of the list (so far; though we are not yet at the stage where my children laugh at my dancing in public).

Of course, none of this would be quite as objectionable if I were reaping some sort of benefit from the presence of Bahain in my community. But while another family two roads up are savouring her babysitting, childminding, cooking and cleaning skills – and all without having to teach her carrot – I am up just one mildly amusing exchange (me: 'When did you come to London?' her: 'Wictoria Station.') and down several English lessons, a dose of dignity and countless conversations about the Hungarian climate, on which topic (and which topic alone) she is surprisingly fluent. Apparently, in her bit of the Balkans, winters are very harsh but rarely wet. While Bahain has learnt the names of several vegetables, three bus routes, most of the London Underground System and a classic children's song from me, this is the single piece of information I have gleaned from her. And she hasn't even washed so much as a cup.

Still, if there is one thing the perpetually smiling Bahain has taught me – albeit quite by accident – it is that this whole au pair game isn't all it's cracked up to be. Poor mouth aside, the whole idea of a Bahain grinning in my home twenty-four hours a day – even with a tea-towel in her hand – is not an attractive one. There are certain things that a family simply can't comfortably do in front of strangers: fart, scratch each other, hit the children, wander around in bad or no underwear, and it is this whole best behaviour business that would ultimately send me screaming off to Eastern Europe. Besides which, I've observed enough au pairs in the playground over the years to know that the official au pair attitude to children is benevolent and obliging until the day that the floundering girl meets another au pair, at which point she loses all interest in the children and devotes all her playground hours to smoking, while her shivering and soaking charges beg to be allowed go home.

All that, and your husband will run off with her given half the chance. Now next time Bahain's benign *bean an tí* gushes about how great she is with a grater, how her finger puppets outshine all others and how her English is coming on a treat, I just have to remember all that. Even if it is through gritted teeth.

PARENT-TEACHER MEETING

SMALL GIRL: 3 YEARS, 6 MONTHS
BOY: 1 YEAR, 5 MONTHS

While I haven't exactly spent the past few years fantasising about my first parent-teacher meeting, I must confess that any time the prospect did flicker past my mind's eye, it usually involved the words Oxford, Cambridge and Prodigy being bandied about to the accompaniment of some vigorous hand-shaking and a great deal of back-slapping. But somehow, between conception and three-and-a-half, The Small Girl has decided to chart a slightly different course through life than the one her gifted parents had mapped for her. And so it was that two grown educators had to have a twenty-minute discussion on how best to describe a problem child without using the word problem before they could even look me in the eye last Tuesday evening.

In fairness to The Small Girl, my own role in the fantasy parent-teacher meeting was also seriously undermined – in this case by the fact that the encounter took place in a classroom. In my head, I was always steered directly to the principal's office, the better to share sherry and the wonderment of my micro-genius. Call me immature, but too many excited evenings of school concerts and extra-curricular skylarking have meant that I still find the prospect of being in a classroom after dark a tantalising, almost illicit pleasure, and so while The Small Girl's teachers struggled to find their words, I conducted a more silent battle to smother the urge to draw a pair of breasts on the blackboard, write 'FL was here' underneath it and then run out of the room with my jumper over my head. Come to think of it, perhaps Oxford was a tad optimistic.

But we're not giving up just yet. The problem with the girl, it appears, is that she's decided that formal education is not for her and finds herself unable to explain why. 'But I don't like nursery school' has become something of a mantra in our home of late, and every known form of child psychology – and a few I've made up myself – have failed to elicit any more elaborate reason for her unhappiness at the chalkface. I could go on about this for several more pages (oh, who am I kidding; volumes), but frankly, it's not terribly funny and since there's no real resolution to it, I'll just move on to the positive aspect of the parent-teacher meeting: our daughter is one of the best in the class at cutting-out (we're so proud, we could burst) and then I'll draw a line under her and start talking about The Boy instead.

In actual fact, The Boy may well be part of The Small Girl's problems (or complexities, as her teachers prefer to call them). While she's been bubbling away beautifully, developing into what I had, until recently, assumed was a perfectly happy child with only a rather disturbing obsession with *The Sound of Music* to suggest the trouble ahead, The Boy has been quietly turning into a man mountain whose principal aim in life is to systematically destroy whatever his sister is up to. If it is any consolation to her (and it isn't), his powers of mass destruction are not limited to The Small Girl's world – her first visit to the library ended in tears because there were 'too many books'; his finished badly because there were too many chairs, and he'd already thrown three of them into the teenage section and a fourth had damaged Beatrix Potter irreparably.

In addition to his superhuman strength and an occasionally impressive ability to withstand very high temperatures, like the grill, he remains a miserable individual to most comers. While The Small Girl had more than thirty words at eighteen months (I wrote them down; you do that before teachers destroy your dreams), his sole means of communication appears to be punching people in the face.

But my God, he loves his mammy. In bed with me in the tiny hours, The Boy will whisper all the words he won't say aloud for anyone else, and he'll snuggle so close that after we've both nodded off again, we need to be peeled apart. It's not just a special relationship, it's a whole secret world that I'm determined to enjoy for as long as I'm let. The time will come when he won't even want to be in the same room as me, let alone the same bed, and so I'm loving every inch of my lovely, cuddly boy. Yesterday, in my intensive kissing of him, I felt his Adam's apple for the first time and it almost made me cry. Five minutes later he stole his sister's apple and hit her over the head with it for the umpteenth time and it made her cry, while the resultant smack from me made him cry. My God, this parenting business has its complexities.

COMING HOME

SMALL GIRL: 3 YEARS, 7 MONTHS
BOY: 1 YEAR, 6 MONTHS

And so, almost nine months to the day that we first put our home on the market, we are finally about to be delivered of it. By the time you read this, ferries and fortune permitting, we will be home.

In the meantime, there are several small mountains to be scaled. The first is the most literal: cardboard towers have grown up all over our flat – the 'Dublin boxes' designed for everything except climbing on, and at the moment, used for little else. Consequently, in tandem with the Dublin boxes have come the Dublin threats – as in 'leave that alone or we'll go to Dublin without you' and sundry other shockers that may well arise again in therapy in years to come. If they do, we shall plead extenuating circumstances; in keeping with all the clichés about moving house being the most stressful business after bereavement and divorce, these past few weeks have been teeth- and cheek-clenchers of the highest order.

It started well enough – and to be honest, as it nears its completion, it has been a fairly bog-standard exercise in buying and selling – but as time has ticked by and delays, disruptions, setbacks and hiccups have mounted up, it's become akin to a psychological thriller in which blood-curdling catastrophe always lurks around the corner but never quite takes a bite. In keeping with the waking nightmare image, I have also, for sport, given up sleeping. These nights I count cardboard boxes, worry about unreliable removals vans, tardy solicitors (the legal eagles we are using in London value their lunchbreak and scarcely inspire confidence; also, I'm almost certain I've spotted *The Little Book of Law* on their tatty shelves), I envisage buyers changing their minds, banks changing their terms, and, last night, for a laugh, sinking car ferries. By 6am, and having exhausted every possible improbability, I am ready for sleep and drift off for those precious few minutes before The Boy decides to herald the dawn and unpack a few more boxes. Overall, I'm not sure I'm taking this very well.

Inevitably, it would be a deal easier if we didn't have the exchange rate to contend with. For seven years I have lived with the consequences of a strong pound, seeing my Irish wages flitter down to nothing in a stroke of the calculator. All this, though, was borne with good grace in anticipation of the Pay-Off; the day on which we sold our flat and turned the sterling profit into punts in abundance. But it seems that while interest rates rose and fell, budgets came and went and whole administrations changed, nothing has had quite as dramatic an effect on the value of sterling as The Husband and I finding a house and uttering the magical words 'we'll take it'. On that halcyon day, just over two months ago, sterling was higher than it's ever been, but as the breath left our lips, it began its blissful freefall towards earth and parity. It could have been far worse – and for a couple of weeks it looked distinctly as though it would be far worse – and those were the longest days and shortest nights of all.

But now we are down to decimal points and, a complete stock-market collapse within the next three days notwithstanding (and don't think I haven't considered that in the small hours), the children won't starve. Indeed, The Boy won't even notice; his time in London lost to an undeveloped long-term memory. The Small Girl, who in many respects is the most settled and rooted of all of us here, is 'a little bit sad and a little bit happy', but overall anxious to become a Dublin girl with her own bedroom in our big new Dublin house.

Me, I just wish we'd gone up to Ally Pally one more time when the sun was shining. I wish we'd made that trip to Bath, visited Portobello Market on a Saturday and ridden the London Eye. I wish I'd taken more photographs, eaten in more restaurants and been to the doctor for free a few more times. Those are the regrets. On the starboard side, I'm looking forward to defying common sense by getting off buses at the front again, I've always liked the sound of our pound coins better than theirs, and I do relish the prospect of The Small Girl losing her London accent. I miss

Brennan's bread and chocolate Kimberleys and pubs that don't throw their customers out just to comply with a few pesky regulations. I have done my tour of duty; I have occupied British soil for seven years as a direct reprisal for what they did to ours, and I can do no more. Maritime disasters notwithstanding, it's time to come home.

ALMOST THERE

SMALL GIRL: 3 YEARS, 7 MONTHS
BOY: 1 YEAR, 6 MONTHS

If we are not quite home, then at least we are back. To be more specific, we are halfway through the Big Move; our hands have been washed of London and all its works and all its empty promises, but we have yet to shake out the welcome mat on our shiny new doorstep. Our stuff (since inquirers seem to have a strange, almost pathological interest in the matter) is in Derry, we are in the parents' home and The Husband, quite sensibly, has gone back.

So while he is commuting, the rest of us are twiddling our thumbs, pestering our solicitor, being depressed about the amount of money we made on the currency exchange and generally wondering if time could possibly move any slower.

The Small Girl, at least, has the much-touted New Dublin School to fill her days. It is going, like so many other aspects of this move, as well as can be expected. Every day she comes home with a new number card in her lunchbox and since they are still in the realm of the ones she already knows, I relax a little. Then I notice Irish words on a poster on her classroom wall and wonder what she is to make of it all.

Meanwhile, in the time that she is becoming bilingual in a London accent, I'm walking round Dunnes Stores trying not to compare prices and – given our national inferiority complex where perfidious Albion is concerned – *really* trying not to tell everyone the results. (Though it is worth pointing out that had I been fully aware of the cost of nappies in these extremities before the big heave-ho, we might have settled on a more modestly priced house.)

Still, as I tell myself a dozen times a day, this is no time for looking back. In particular, the events of last weekend are best buried – if only for the sake of my sanity. But in the interest of good order and mild amusement at the expense of myself and my family, one more time with feeling.

To cut an epic saga down to a poignant paragraph, our fears that we had seriously underestimated the amount of stuff we had and were flying several miles over our own inventory came to nothing when our removals company sent a juggernaut to shift the contents of our two-bedroomed flat.

Indeed, so big was our lorry that all of Crouch End could have moved in it, and since it got stuck three narrow roads away and blocked the North London traffic for a whole day, I understand that many of them considered it.

In the end, we (*we*) paid for a second removal van to come up and shuttle our furniture up to the juggernaut which we (*we*) also had to pay for and eventually, some five hours behind schedule, we wished our world Godspeed and headed ferry-wards. The rest of the adventure can be summed up thus: two major traffic accidents on the motorway resulting in delays of two-and-a-half hours, a car that burst into flames right beside us in a queue, a Burger King that had closed down and an hysterical child who suddenly decided that, after all the bravado and bluster, she just really wanted to go home.

The following afternoon, on the deck of the car ferry and with Wales disappearing to my left and Howth emerging to starboard, I did the only appropriate thing under the circumstances and burst into unstoppable floods of tears. At the time of writing, we've no idea when we'll get into our new house but in the meantime, we are very rich and quite miserable.

But there are little glimmers of sunlight. Like the moment when the New Dublin School teacher handed over The Small Girl at the end of her first morning and called me a mammy instead of the mummy I've been for three-and-a-half years. In these troubled times, whatever they pay Montessori teachers, it isn't half enough.

MY SO-CALLED GLAMOROUS LIFE

SMALL GIRL: 3 YEARS, 8 MONTHS
BOY: 1 YEAR, 7 MONTHS

I have just had my first play broadcast by RTÉ Radio. I enjoyed that so much, I think I'll sum up the main points again: me, play, broadcast. I would have primed you last week but I didn't want to appear immodest/desperate, and also, I hadn't heard it myself then and I couldn't be sure that it hadn't, shall we say, lost something in the mix.

The last time I bragged about one of my extra-curriculars, it managed, through some cack-handed script editing, to turn into the pilot for the hugely unpopular television series, 'Read All Over', so this time I decided to approach with extreme caution. As it was (and I admit to extreme subjectivity here), RTÉ and producer Daniel Reardon in particular, made a more than decent stab at it, so that the broadcast play sounded to the writer (*me!*) much the same as it had sounded in my (*my!*) head.

Joe Taylor played the demanding lead exactly as it was when I (*I!*) made it so demanding, and afterwards we clinked champagne glasses till late in the night, pausing only to snort cocaine off the naked backs of the Leeson Street lap dancers RTÉ had hired en masse for the night and to (begrudgingly) grant sexual favours to Louis Walsh's latest boy band and Bryan Dobson.

At least, much like Joe's interpretation, that's how I thought it should be. In fact, I only knew that the damn thing had even been made because a phone call informed me that the play had a) been recorded; b) that they had had a great laugh doing it; and c) that it was going out the following Tuesday night. And all without me talking about motivation, scribbling directions in the margin or having a single hissy fit. So much for the creative process.

I am reminded (oh, how I have longed to write these words) of William Goldman's depressingly frank book, *Adventures in the Screen Trade*, in which the author explains why the writer – that is, the person who dreams up the idea and brings it to life – is perched precariously upon the lowest rung of the ladder when the production process kicks in. In my case, I had no input into who would bring my characters to life, nor had I any input into how they might sound. But hey, that, apparently, is showbiz.

But what the hell. Me. Play. Broadcast. The excitement in my head – if not my home – was palpable for a week before it was aired and was boosted when *The Irish Times* said lovely things about it in preview.

On Sunday, my entire family came around for dinner and I read the preview aloud (they politely declined to listen to the actual play) and everyone cheered. Then one of my sisters noticed – where my giddy head had not – that *The Irish Times* had actually recommended a play called 'Golf Windows', while my opus was called 'Golf Widows'. It made the beef momentarily more chewy but it couldn't quite dispel the notion that in some small way and to some inconsequential place, I had arrived.

And so, showtime. On Tuesday morning, the producer phoned to remind me that tonight was my big night. In the afternoon, I called to my parents' home and gently reminded them too that tonight was the night. Oh dear, they collectively exclaimed: they had watched the first part of a (not very good – their words) drama on BBC1 the previous night and were looking forward to watching its conclusion at the same time as their daughter's first play received its world premiere. I excused them and headed for home and my own big night.

It goes without saying that I heard not a single word of my first play ('hilarious' – *The Irish Times*) being broadcast. The Husband being about his commuting business, I spent my hour of hours on my night of nights reading a poxy book about the Teletubbies and a stupid fucking lamb twenty times to my pain-in-the-arse son when I should have been drinking Cristal champagne out of Hugh Leonard's loafer, or some such.

I only knew it was over because my parents rang (thank the Lord for video tapes) so that my father could ask me the all-important question: how long had it taken me to write it (and by inference, why?) Well, it took me long enough. And whatever the circumstances of its premiere, in my head, I was having a party. Me, Daniel Reardon, Joe Taylor, the rest of the cast and crew, my family and friends. And what the hell, the lap dancers, the boy band and Bryan Dobson too. After all, it's not every day that you have a play. Broadcast. Me.

HOME IMPROVEMENTS

SMALL GIRL: 3 YEARS, 9 MONTHS
BOY: 1 YEAR, 8 MONTHS

Our 1970's house is gradually disappearing beneath a veneer of maple. Over the past four weeks, we have knocked down one wall, built another one, removed a fireplace, five carpets, a mustard-coloured kitchen and a pair of curtains that awakened in me a violent streak I never knew existed. On the credit side (in every sense), we have fitted a new kitchen and a new floor, stripped and sanded two others and done something a bit arty with the hole where the fireplace used to be and a load of candles. The picture of The Sacred Heart we have kept, because I was afraid not to. Oh yes, and we've insulated the attic, fixed the central heating system and installed enough television points to ensure our marriage lasts forever.

I say 'we', but of course, 'we' have done very little aside from engage in the kind of international diplomacy that's required when a whole family has to live in a single room for weeks on end. The real graft has been done by Noel, Phil, two Micks, Brian, Frank, Dave, Gerry and two young lads whose names I didn't catch because they brought their own sound system and cranked it to the max even as they cracked open their first tube of floor glue. It is a credit to Sanyo that we could still hear their jungle rhythms over two electric saws and a crying baby.

There were also two men in the attic but since I hardly saw them, I can't really count them. For all I know, they may still be there. If they are, then perhaps I might pass them up one of the

Mick's trowels, Phil's paint scraper, Frank's screwdriver, half a worktop, the same Mick's cup and the rest of the materials that have been left behind, to see what they might come up with. If it is a way of removing the wallpaper that the previous owners appear to have superglued to the walls, we might even consider letting them out before Phase Two of the modernisation of the 1970's house begins in earnest.

That is scheduled – in case they're reading this through a crack in the ceiling – for whenever we get more money. In the meantime, we need to let the dust settle on Phase One. And boy, is there dust. It seems that a Phil, a Noel or a Mick only has to ring the doorbell for a thick cloud of the stuff to descend on the ground floor and all that resides on it. It is everywhere: in cups, on curtains, in pieces of Lego and in and on the ever-increasing pile of bin bags outside our back door. Yesterday, I found some in the turn-ups of my jeans. Had I known that doing up our new home would result in one-room living conditions evocative of *Angela's Ashes* – with the ashes themselves swirling around our ankles – then I might have made it my business to develop a soft spot for mustard melamine.

But there are pinpricks of brightness beginning to emerge from the dusty sheath and our new kitchen is almost a joy to behold. While other rooms in the house have yet to find their wow factor, the kitchen is actually improving with age, so much so that by the time it's as hopelessly unfashionable as its predecessor, I may well have married it on 'The Jerry Springer Show'.

That is, if I can find some time off from cleaning the damn thing. Once upon a time, I had a hob, an oven and a floor and all they needed to make us all shine was a bottle of Jif. Now Jif has become Cif and one bottle has become an armload of new cleaning potions and methods. We have rationalised it now so that the soft pink cloth is for shining the oven door, the soft yellow cloth is for the hob and the white cloth that goes on the end of a handle is for the floor. Then there is soapy wood cleaner, not to be allowed dry in, ceramic hob cleaner, not to be applied when warm, chrome oven polish, not to be applied by me because (according to The Husband) I haven't got the wrist for it, and a variety of back-up scrapers and grease takers should all the above fail to eradicate the evidence of people ever having lived here.

Because all of the above is hugely time-consuming, we are eating a lot of takeaways. Now, if I can just persuade the chipper to take in our washing and let the kids play on their floor while I try to avoid walking on mine, then we might just have the kitchen of my dreams.

THREE LITTLE WORDS

SMALL GIRL: 3 YEARS, 9 MONTHS
BOY: 1 YEAR, 8 MONTHS

The world has lost some of its sheen. The Small Girl has told me that she hates me. My dramatic tumble in her estimation was caused, for the record, by my being bound by the laws of physics and therefore unable to stand a three-inch doll on top of a four-inch pony and insert the result onto the middle floor of her brother's toy garage. The immediate after-effect of the declaration of hostilities was a three-and-a-half year old sitting in her pyjamas happily inserting a more pliable Bob The Builder into the garage while singing 'If You're Happy and You Know It' and an eejit of a mother slumped over the table contemplating a soggy piece of toast through tear-filled eyes.

I am not proud of the following: that I spent the next ten minutes mentally listing all the hardships I'd endured to get The Small Girl into this world and a position where she could even *consider* populating a small garage; that I then *pointed these hardships out to her*; and that I told the other mothers outside the playgroup what my ungrateful daughter had said. I was vaguely relieved when one of them kindly asked if this was my first time while the rest of them just laughed at me. And I was entirely relieved that The Small Girl didn't seem to pay too much notice to my cataloguing of the woes she's wreaked upon my head.

I have always regarded the country song 'No Charge' – in which a child attempts to earn some honest pocket-money by doing chores and is rebuked by his mother with a keening list of all the unpleasantries she's endured on his behalf and for which there is, predictably, no charge – as a steaming pile of sentimentality. Yet here I was, that mother, weighing up the cost of my own near death at my daughter's birth, the three weeks I watched over her in intensive care and all the shit that has happened since, and wondering why it hadn't compensated in her small world for my inability to place a seven-inch amalgamation of pony and Polly Pocket into a five-inch confined space.

But, at least for those few minutes, it obviously hadn't. At approximately 8.05am last Tuesday morning, I entered my daughter's top ten hates charts, straight in at number one. Amongst those giving chase were cheese, shampoo, her father's choice of television programmes, her old runners and a boy called Charlie (whose mother once invited me to her home so that she could flog me jewellery and who, consequently, I also hate).

Of course, a year ago, The Small Girl didn't hate anything. Play-school – first in London and now in Dublin – has introduced her to a world of delights and turned her from a baby into a confident child and occasional madam, but it has also taught her – however briefly and indiscriminately – how to hate. Now, for every episode of 'Barney', there is an equal and opposite instalment of 'Time Team' or another of her dad's programmes to ruin her day. For each piece of chalk there is a slice of cheese and for every moment of mild heroics on my part, there is some deep flaw in my abilities.

Her plastic cup is not quite half empty, but there are times when she looks at it and it certainly isn't half full. She has now begun a journey that will almost inevitably lead her to a high-voiced pro-test outside the Dáil when she is sixteen and her teachers are revolting.

In the meantime, though, the good news is that I'm top of the pops again. It's difficult to put my finger on what precisely pro-pelled me back into the good books, but by the time I handed her over to the authorities at the playschool a scant hour after her dec-laration of loathing, The Small Girl had told me she loved me again. Out of sheer embarrassment, I hope it wasn't the 'I carried you for nine months ...' dirge that brought about the sudden change of heart. It is one thing to have your three-and-a-half year old daughter hate you, but quite another to have her suspect you of being mad.

Besides, I understand from the old lags outside the school that there are many more declarations of hostilities ahead. If I am to perform an inventory of my pains and scars each time, neither of us will ever get anything done, the toy garage will go out of busi-ness and I won't have time to dwell on how much I really hate the fitters who made such a hames of our kitchen floor. And as The Small Girl might say, I hate that.

SWAN DIVES

SMALL GIRL: 3 YEARS, 11 MONTHS
BOY: 1 YEAR, 10 MONTHS

Now here's a sentence I never thought I'd write: I have just been attacked by a swan. If this was television, it's at this point that I would drop my trousers in order that (after your initial mixture of confusion, panic and embarrassment) you could admire the strap of a black bruise that stretches right across my upper thigh, courtesy of my long-necked assailant. As it is, you'll simply have to take my word for it – I had a fight with a swan, and on points, he won. And while he has presumably now resumed his bullying ways, I may never be the same again. I am, in many respects, the Lennox Lewis of swan fighting.

The bout, let the records show, took place in my local park, to which I'd taken the kids for a gambol and a dispersing of stale heels of Brennan's bread amongst the waterfowl. The birds, for the most part, were the usual mixture of ravenously hungry and utterly disinterested, with the pair of swans that rules the roost there registering somewhere between the two. As the last crumbs fell into the water, though, the swan that had been indulging us to some degree suddenly left the pond, made for The Boy – who was just standing there minding his own business – and in a beat, had taken his chubby hand in its beak.

What happened next probably took just a couple of seconds, but in my mind's eye it lasted for days. The Boy started screaming, I joined in, a scant octave higher, I tried to pull The Boy's hand out of the swan's mouth and, failing that, I whacked the bastard hard across his preposterous neck. This was enough to make him release The Boy and turn his attention instead to me, which he did by belting me across the thigh with what I think was probably his wing but felt like a lead girder. With a speed and sleight of hand previously unknown to myself, I then scooped up The Boy, grabbed The Small Girl's hand and took off, shouting at the bewildered girl – who had missed the action by dint of her having her head in the empty Brennan's bread bag – to run. And so we ran, me in my high-heeled boots clutching a 30lb boy and a small girl, and the swan, a peck behind us, in hot pursuit. Under the circumstances, I did the only thing possible: I turned my head towards our pursuer and screamed at him to 'fuck off' at the top of my voice and several times over.

Needless to say, it was only at this point that the fracas received any attention from our fellow gambollers, who turned to witness a grown woman running in an ungainly fashion from a swan while simultaneously verbally abusing it. I can't really blame anyone for not intervening; though I might take issue with the man who laughed so much he had an asthma attack.

Of course, it could have been worse. A swan can break your arm, as 10,000 people have been happy to inform me since the incident. Also, they're inclined to be very vicious if their young are threatened. Well, so can I – and since this particular winged avenger didn't even *have* kids (I hate to sound smug, but there you go), I think I had the higher moral ground on this one. Plus, The Boy, who is completely capable of working cats and dogs into a frenzy with his own excitement levels, had been doing nothing; just standing there, sharing his pitiful few crumbs with this big bloody bully.

So the upshot of all this is that I'm now trying my damnedest to bring Foot and Mouth disease into my locale, to modify the disease in some ingenious way so that it bothers the webbed as well as the cloven-footed and to visit it upon that big white fucker in the park. Even if I can only achieve the first two of these ambitions, I can surely arrange to have my long-necked nemesis culled, which would suit me just fine. In fact, I'll be happy to scale the walls of Tymon Park and carry out the slaughter myself, thigh permitting. Word has it that the Royals are partial to a bit of swan steak – and I'd be proud to carry that particular royal appointment. In the meantime, if there are any other waterfowl who are feeling lucky, let them take notice that you mess with The Boy, you mess with his mother. He may be an ugly duckling, but he is my ugly duckling, and under my protection, he too will grow into a swan. After all, you are what you eat.

TOILET TROUBLES

SMALL GIRL: 3 YEARS, 11 MONTHS
BOY: 1 YEAR, 10 MONTHS

There comes a time in every man's life when he needs to take control of his destiny. But first, he needs to have a handle on his bowels. That's the message we're currently trying to convey to The Boy, whose toilet habits are rapidly becoming less an occasionally sweet sideline of babyhood and more of a public health issue. Put it this way: he is some way off being a blue flag candidate and if the warm weather keeps up, he may have to be sealed off completely. More than that, you do not need to know.

Though obviously, I'm still going to tell you. The most extraordinary – and indeed baffling – difference between our two children is that while The Small Girl is a petite package of loveliness, a fortnight short of four years and still running around in shorts labelled 6-12 months, The Boy is a monstrosity: a gargantuan mass who, at twenty-two months, weighs more than his sister, has bigger and smellier feet and easily passes for three-and-a-half. Still, the fact that I seem to spend a great deal of my life mollifying strangers who can't extract a satisfactory answer to the traditional 'and how old are you?' inquisition from The Boy doesn't bother me half as much as his continuing relationship with nappies. It is unfair to expect any child – especially any boy – to be an under-panted impresario before he is two, but when he looks and smells like twice the man he is, then the whole business of soiling oneself becomes, well, a significant pain in the arse.

And never was it more acute than last weekend, when an evacuation in the living room was followed, mere minutes later, by an intoxicating encore on the bus. Since I've already arguably gone into far too much detail on this, I won't dwell on the environ-mental impact of The Boy poring forth on the bus, but suffice to say, there were a lot of people very grateful to get to their destina-tion last Saturday. Unfortunately for us, our own destination was the city centre, which had promised belated St Patrick's Festival high jinks but, as far as we could see, delivered little more than a procession of profanities. Admittedly, many of them were my own – the first when two chemist shops on O'Connell Street reacted to my request to purchase nappies and baby wipes as though I had demanded a nuclear missile and a small hedgehog – as were most of the subsequent ones when every suitable shop from there to the far end of Grafton Street elected to follow suit.

Now, I know this is my boy, my bee and my bonnet, but indulge me here: isn't it reasonable to expect chemist shops to sell nappies? And small supermarkets like Spar and Centra, fully armed with emergency supplies of hair conditioner – would it be too much to ask that they might also have something in the arse-wiping department? Well, no and yes would appear to be the answers to those particular Fair City riddles, since I ended up, Boy in tow, getting all the way to Dunnes Stores in the St Stephen's Green Centre before finally finding something with which to restore public order. As a postscript to this malodorous adventure, the baby-changing facilities in Dunnes were, of course, closed, and eventually, the dirty deed was done in Mothercare, which we'd already visited in order to discover that the world- famous baby shop sells nipple shields, but not nappies.

But back to the unseasonal festivities. The Saturday afternoon street carnival was, even by very low standards, extremely poor and consisted mainly of an oversized dirigible with a big ball on it and something terribly complicated concerning the seven deadly sins. This, and the rest of the handful of feeble attractions, prompted the good burghers of Dublin to mutter things like 'What the fuck is that?', 'Who's that fuckin' eejit?', 'This is shite', and, from the especially articulate, 'This is fuckin' shite', as they shuffled past. They were right to a man, and the whole spectacle served only to remind me that while we might like to think we are the new Barcelona, our real claim to international fame is our world-beating swearing.

Of course, there are those who would say that a decent and responsible mother would never leave home without nappies, but frankly, I am not now, nor have I ever been, that kind of mother. Besides which, my continuing mid-life crisis has just led me to a fairly radical change of hair style and colour that has left me looking uncannily like Geri Halliwell. Unfortunately, it is the old Geri Halliwell, but with the new breasts. And you think I've got time to worry about packing nappies?

FIGHTING IN FOREIGN PARTS

SMALL GIRL: 4 YEARS, 1 MONTH
BOY: 2 YEARS

The holiday went as well as could be expected, given that our children declared war on each other moments before the taxi arrived to take us to the airport. At the time of writing, they are still awaiting the appointment of a miniature George Mitchell-type figure to help them come to some agreement, but like David Trimble, we're not hopeful.

The reason for this outbreak of hostilities remains a mystery, but the shape of the fight has been all too predictable. The Boy, boasting a superior fighting weight, almost invariably starts each round with a spate of unwieldy punching followed by some more precise pinching. The Small Girl, weary to her tiny core and pinched to the point of no return, retaliates with a single well-placed bite. She then retires to her corner to whine about the pinching while her opponent hits the canvas in a fit of uncontrollable grief. At this point the referee enters the ring, scoops up the disappointed Boy, insists that it serves him right, demands The Small Girl stop whinging and protests (quite pointlessly and a tad pathetically) that it's 'Mammy and Daddy's holiday too'. The second official then intervenes, chastising The Boy so severely as to prompt a fresh bout of tears and ordering all parties to 'be nice to Mammy' so that Mammy begins to wonder if Daddy knows something she doesn't. I think I saw a film like this once, and as far as I can remember, it ended with a funeral. Still, in many ways, it was a happy release.

The only respite from the fighting comes in the shape of the

Budget Travel Kiddies Club. Quite sensibly, they refuse to touch The Boy with a barge pole. But the Girl, a breath over the requisite four years old, is welcomed to a yellow world of fun and games by a couple of gamey young people who promise her so much fun it'll make her puke (I'm paraphrasing). Unfortunately, Day Two is video day. When a silent Small Girl returns to our apartment and hangs up her yellow hat, we manage to coax from her that she has seen a 'people's film' (as distinct from a 'girl's film') about a man who 'goes to a football match and kills everyone'. She will not, she informs us, be requiring the services of the Kiddies Club again.

She is convinced to give it a second chance by her father ('be nice to Mammy'), and eventually I discover that the offending film was not *McVicar* (as I had believed), but something called *The Waterboy*, in which, by all accounts, a man goes to a football match and kills everyone. That issue resolved, the fun and games recommence, reaching a dizzy height on the Friday night with a performance of *Grease* in which The Small Girl stars as the Pink Lady who stands very still and looks startled. Elsewhere on the stage, Sandy is played by a pubescent girl who towers over a miniature and terrified Danny. The relevant parents are proud as punch, while we just wonder afresh if our firstborn – so utterly fazed by Rydell High – is really ready for Bishop Shanahan Primary. Still, when she almost falls off the stage at the end she elicits a wave of cutesy 'aahs' so all may not be lost. If school doesn't work out, then a lucrative career on 'You've Been Framed' may be in the offing.

The Boy, meanwhile, went from bad to worse, so much so that at the end of the holiday, the proprietor of the apartments caught me calling him an arsehole, which wouldn't have been so bad if the aforementioned arsehole hadn't been fast asleep at the time. In between, we had endured spectacular bad behaviour, a couple of atrocious accidents, a dozen ruined evening meals and an ungainly fall into the deep end of the pool. Other than that though, like Mrs Lincoln, we had a perfectly lovely time.

Indeed, what with the Be Nice To Mammy policy and some skin-singeing sunshine, it would have been perfectly sublime if it hadn't been for our own children and one of somebody else's – a specimen of about ten years of age in a Manchester United top who spent the two weeks circumnavigating the pool on one of those absurd silver scooters which (get this) was fitted with a device which rang like a mobile phone every time its rider completed a lap. It occurred to me, as I tried to concentrate on my critically-acclaimed book, that this child might well have been the most annoying in the whole world, and in that light, our own Boy didn't look so bad. In fact, in the middle of his daily siesta, he looked almost loveable. For an arsehole.

BIRTHDAY PARTIES

SMALL GIRL: 4 YEARS, 1 MONTH
BOY: 2 YEARS

Becoming the first people in history to emigrate from England to Ireland for economic reasons is something to tell the grandchildren; that we did so principally because we were financially unable to keep up with the London birthday party circuit is something we might keep a deal quieter. It is one thing to be squeezed out of a country by escalating property prices and punitive taxes, but is quite another to be chased away by a bulging party bag and a clown called Tootles.

But the grim reality is that London is in the grip of a children's party nightmare. As heroin was to Dublin in the 1980s, so children's birthday parties are to North London in the new millennium. Initially seductive, what began as a harmless distraction has escalated into a most invidious addiction – empty, unsatisfactory and, of course, prohibitively expensive. For my part, I can only give thanks that I got out when I did. Had I stayed, by now I would have been robbing old ladies' handbags on Crouch End Broadway just to feed my children's party habit.

It started innocently enough. But even at the beginning, there were subtle signs of the full-scale madness to come. I did wonder, when everyone around me hosted birthday parties for their one-year-olds, if the festivities weren't a tad premature. The joy of having a one- and indeed a two-year old, is, surely, that they are sublimely clueless about pretty much everything – and to burden them with complex notions like time seems to me unfair. Far better, we thought, to let the first two birthdays pass with the minimum of ceremony and present buying. So, on The Small Girl's first anniversary, I splashed out on a chocolate bun, stuck a candle in it and ate it myself. While all around her, little Joshuas and Ellas were being toasted in McDonald's and serenaded by strangers, our daughter spent the day in quiet reflection.

She was also the only child in our area not to have a second birthday party. But Lordy, she went to plenty. By then, Clown Town – a local soft play centre, not dissimilar to Beirut – had become the party venue of choice, as whole legions of wobbly two-year-olds queued up to receive treats from a bunch of surly clowns dreaming of better things, like a prison sentence. At three, I acknowledged that it would be cruel to continue keeping her birthday a secret from her, and so we had our first proper fix: a mainline dose of party pleasure, complete with party bags, pass the parcel and petulant guests. But of course, it wasn't enough. The girl down the road had a clown, her neighbour had a puppet show and almost every other three-year-old had a bouncy castle. And at each celebration, the party bag grew. The Small Girl's goody bags had sent all-comers home with a lollipop, a deflated balloon and a gizmo from a Woolworth's Big Bag Of Worthless Gizmos. By the time of Abigail's party (honestly) and the end of the season, the bags had swelled to veritable sacks, groaning with sweets, treats, proper toys, notebooks, jewellery, hair accessories and almost always came attached to a shiny helium balloon in the shape of somebody off the telly. It was after Abigail's party that we knew we had to get out.

Six months later, six months clean, we returned last week to our old manor. The bad news is that the boat on the Thames hired for one of the Joshuas' fourth birthday is unavailable on the Sunday, so the party's on the Friday. The good news is that Rachel's found a party co-ordinator for Holly's big four, and she only charges £150 for her services. The clown that everyone used last year has left town – presumably to retire to the south of France – but there's a local magician who throws in a puppet show for £200. Meanwhile, Daniel has seen off his second birthday in a bouncy castle that turned out to be slightly bigger than his garden, while his mother has spent the last three months waking up in the night thinking of more things to put in her daughter's party bag come the glorious day next month. To this end, she's ordered several dozen toys from a mail order catalogue. Rachel thinks she should join Party Bags Anonymous.

Meanwhile, The Small Girl went to her first Irish birthday party and came home, mercifully, with a party bag containing a lollipop and a black jack. For her own birthday last month, I significantly upped the ante by adding to each bag a hair accessory, a chocolate bar and a small packet of sweets. I just couldn't help myself. Ireland may be in my heart, but the children's birthday parties of North London are in my veins.

TIME TRAVEL

SMALL GIRL: 4 YEARS, 1 MONTH
BOY: 2 YEARS

It was while sitting up in bed joining The Boy in a robust version of 'Postman Pat' at 4.50am the other morning that I unlocked the key to time travel. It didn't come in a blinding flash – in keeping with events outside my bedroom window, it was more of a slow dawn. For the scientific record, I should note that the secret that has eluded mankind since time itself first began to confound him revealed itself to me after umpteen verses eulogising the Postman and between numerous demands for kisses (a development which may yet see our relationship finish up on 'EastEnders'). It happened thus: according to the digital display on the alarm clock beside the bed, The Boy began to sing at 4.44am. Some time later, when every fibre in my body was screaming that a good (if indecent) hour had passed, and that it was time either to get up or begin weeping inconsolably, I checked the clock again. It was 4.50am. While my mind and body had travelled a whole hour, just six minutes of real time had passed. A great light began to dawn.

It occurred to me that this wasn't the only time when the clock had conspicuously failed to keep up with me. Any time I embark on so-called creative play with the children, the clock slows again until its every tick lasts several minutes. Just the other day, we made birthday cards, which, in human years, took four hours to complete, but in physical time occupied only forty-five minutes. This is also true of anything at all that involves glitter, glue, paints or cutting out. By extension, observing The Boy tip a pot of paint over the newly cleaned sofa takes a whole hour; every technicolour detail of it captured in slow motion. But check the clock and – hey presto! – the action has taken no more than a couple of seconds.

This set me thinking. If time is indeed such a flexible commodity, then can we not begin to manipulate it: to slow it down when it suits our purpose and speed it up when we can't be bothered hanging around? And if we can do that, then can we not manipulate it to a point where we can actually move it backwards?

Now, obviously, time travel through the medium of glitter and glue is an absurd notion. So the next step in my quest for the way back to the future was to identify other occasions of moveable time. One very obvious one is housework. Time barely moves at all when you're cleaning the house – and comes to an absolute standstill when you attack the bathroom – but the knowledge that you're doing the housework because somebody important is coming to visit will speed up the passage of time so dramatically that in the same period as you can clean and redecorate an entire house when nobody's coming to call, you'll only have had a chance to put down the Harpic and pick the knickers up off the bedroom floor before there's a ring on the doorbell.

But time never moves more slowly than when you're exercising. It is an acknowledged fact that if a person leaves their house to 'go for a run' and checks their watch a half-an-hour later, they will find that they've been running for four minutes. In fact, the only reason that the big hand will have moved at all is because when you're exercising outside, there are things to look at. Run on a treadmill in a gym with only a blank wall for distraction, and you will find it is possible for your body, your mind and your trainers to age by two hours in just two minutes. And this, my friends, is the key to time travel.

In order to make time actually move backwards, all a traveller has to do is run on a treadmill while conducting a children's arts and crafts session and simultaneously trying to clean a hand basin. By combining these three time-bending disciplines, it will be possible to start off at, say, 4pm and finish, and hour later, at five to. It's a small step, obviously, but more importantly, it's a step backwards. Soon we will be able to build our own time machines from treadmills, Armitage Shanks and fuzzy felt, and then, like Bono, we will all be running to stand still. Think of the possibilities: we will be able to bet on GAA quarter-final draws before they happen, fill in last minute Lottery slips with the benefit of hindsight and postpone closing time until we're good and ready for it.

We will not, as yet, be able to shorten the 'Postman Pat' dawn chorus, but I'm working on it. Time is on my side and then some.

HOME HOLIDAYS

SMALL GIRL: 4 YEARS, 2 MONTHS
BOY: 2 YEARS, 1 MONTH

As far as I'm concerned, all golf is crazy golf, but there's no doubt that some golf is crazier than others. The one at Pirate's Cove in Courtown, for example, is particularly mental. On what is, in effect, a custom-built mini Treasure Island, complete with shipwreck and tantalising caves, visitors are required to tap small balls up and down small slopes and into small holes. There are skulls and treasure chests and exotic wildlife along the way – but the chances are that you'll miss them all, because – like so many people in Courtown – you'll be too busy trying to get your hole in one. I am pleased to report, then, that my family has recently completed the

Pirate's Cove experience without getting a single ball into a single hole. At the end of the course, we handed back our golf sticks and an unblemished score card that we advised the attendant to use again. We may be crazy, but we are none of us golfers.

And it's not as if we told the children to avoid the golf aspect of this golf course. On the contrary, we were willing to suspend our own distaste of the game for an hour and we actively encouraged both the children to tap balls left, right and centre. But The Small Girl was too busy having a great time and looking out for pirates to bother with such distractions, while The Boy just kicked his orange ball all the way around. As to their parents, we declined to partake in any clubbing because a) we think it's beneath us and b) we were too busy having a fight about whether or not to go bowling afterwards.

So there you have it. After the promises, threats and idle budgetary speculation, we have finally taken the plunge: we have holidayed at home. Now, admittedly, this week in Wexford marked the end of a soggy summer that we kicked off with a fortnight in Spain, but I still think we are to be commended by Bord Fáilte for doing our patriotic duty and contributing to the local tourist industry. And it wasn't a completely selfless gesture – I swore, after our recent foreign holidays, that I was done with the Costas. Weary of welcome meetings and addled by airport delays, I have become convinced that holidaying at home is the way ahead. Besides, and in spite of the conventional wisdom, I was sure it must be cheaper.

And you know, it wasn't all bad. We had two days on the beach. Not 'Holy-God-I'm-Dying-Here' days but clement enough to take to the sands, top up the tans and paddle about in the periphery of the Irish Sea. Obviously, anything more ambitious water-wise would have resulted in tragedy – there were people *surfing*, for

God's sake – but the kids were happy, I was able to take most of my clothes off and The Husband got to make a Batmobile in the sand. Of course, we also had three days when it rained without even stopping for breath, and just one with a sulky sky that couldn't decide what to do. That was the Gorey day, on which we discovered that there isn't an awful lot to do in Gorey.

For the rain, we had the shelter of a television – just one of the mod cons in a rented house that was, in many respects, more luxurious than our own (though given the state of the 1970's house, that wouldn't be hard) – and for the bits in between we had Courtown with its slots and … well, with its slots.

In the swimming pool they made us wear silly caps that we could take home to put with our collection of flimsy swimming caps from the leisure centres of Ireland. When I put the hat on The Boy, I made a mental note to remind him in later life not to wear hats; while The Small Girl in a swimming cap looked like something off an ad, The Boy was more like some kind of a grim warning.

On the last night we counted the cost and discovered – as I'd suspected – that the Irish holiday had been considerably cheaper than its counterpart. The only drawbacks, I pointed out to The Husband, were the rain, the sulky sky, the fact that The Boy got stung by a wasp and the rather irritating gap in the holiday catering world between burgers and chips and haute cuisine – something that means you really do have to cook. Other than that, I instructed him, it was just dandy. And for his part, he's *almost* convinced. 'It was fine for a week,' he confirmed, 'But if I had to stay here for two weeks I'd drown myself.' All told, I'm considering it a work in progress.

FIRST DAY AT SCHOOL

SMALL GIRL: 4 YEARS, 3 MONTHS
BOY: 2 YEARS, 2 MONTHS

Well, the sky didn't darken, the veil of the temple wasn't torn in two and what wailing and gnashing of teeth there was came from a most unexpected source. But it is accomplished: The Small Girl has started school.

Still, we hesitated right up till the last moment. She is a summer baby, four but only just, and sometimes I think that if she curled up tightly enough, she could still fit in the palm of my hand. But she knows most of her numbers and some of her letters and eventually, her own enthusiasm for state education swung it. Last Friday, she waved goodbye to the women who mind her in the gym and told them she was off to big school. 'How long is she going for?' one of them asked me. 'Fourteen years,' I answered, somewhat confused. The crèche worker looked horrified. She had assumed – as many people do – that our tiny daughter was barely out of nappies and playgroup fodder, yet here she was, bold as brass, bandying about terms like 'big school'. 'Well,' consoled the recovering crèche worker, 'she can always stay back a year.'

I'm not entirely sure that that's the right attitude with which to approach formal education, but to our immense relief, the first few days have passed without too many indicators of any real inability to keep up. The first day was the hardest, of course: a two-and-a-half hour session several months in the planning that promised and delivered a miniature roller coaster of emotion. The uniform skirt that we'd had to have elastic threaded through just to keep it up, the plait I spent twenty minutes trying to do and eventually, with trembling fingers, abandoned in favour of a ponytail, the pink schoolbag, the jumper down to her little thighs and, eventually, the excited smile when it was time to go – every detail was magnified by the significance of the morning.

Of course, it was all very different in 1971, when Irish education was still largely governed by the hedge school ethos. Back then, we were herded into a gloomy hall in uniforms with enough letting down and letting out in them to last us till our Confirmation. From there we were dispatched, without our parents, to a row of prefabs which I still sometimes dream that I'm being chased through by a giant covered in balloons. Thus installed, we sat – all fifty-three of us on List Three – at bare brown tables with only the distant prospect of a ball of *marla* on Friday for company and the occasional sobs of some of the more sensitive souls breaking the silence that seemed to stretch all the way to Leaving Certificate 1984.

Now they have bricks and blocks and madly colourful toys that come apart and stick together and rainbows and songs and sweets before home time. Sure why wouldn't they want to go to school? I half fancied staying myself, and The Boy, dazzled by so many delights, made it abundantly clear that whatever about his sister, he was more than ready for the whole Low Babies experience. In the end, I dragged him, screaming, weeping and fighting, from her classroom and then quickly lost him again as he headed down another corridor and found a different, more accommodating classroom. Ten minutes later the emergency lollipop, bought to bribe The Small Girl to stay, was invoked to make her brother leave. I tied him up outside and returned to Room 4, where the mothers were all issuing variations on the same instructions: 'If you need a wee-wee ask the teacher; if you need a poo (please God don't let them need a poo), don't forget to wipe your bum; if you're too hot take off your jumper.' In a corner, the fathers were admiring a digital camera one of their number had brought to record the historical event and talking about the new iBook. It was clearly time to go. I gave The Small Girl a final hug, whispered that I was very proud of her and, feeling my voice crack, left her to her education.

So I nearly cried, her brother wept for Ireland and she didn't even sigh. On the news at teatime, while she happily made up a song about going to school and stuck her coloured-in fish on the fridge, I watched her four-year-old contemporaries in the Ardoyne being bullied by hateful adults and hurried along by armed soldiers and I almost cried again. And last thing before she closed her eyes, she turned to her beloved doll, Betty, and told her, gravely: 'I'm a big girl now but I'll still always be your Mammy.' And that, I'm afraid, was where the voice went completely and Aughrim was lost.

PET PRESSURES

SMALL GIRL: 4 YEARS, 4 MONTHS
BOY: 2 YEARS, 3 MONTHS

We are coming under intense pressure to get a pet. Next door's cat has become a semi-permanent fixture on our sofa, much to the delight of the children and the pharmacist, whose sales of antihistamines have risen accordingly. I am energetically allergic to our houseguest and all his kind – and since Mog Next Door is a particularly long-haired specimen, I spend most of my days trying to focus through slitted eyes and breathe through streaming nostrils. If you saw the woman who was allergic to horsehair on 'Casualty' last weekend, you'll have a good idea of my general demeanour. If you didn't, then just imagine what Barbara Cartland might have looked like had somebody inflated her with a bicycle pump and you're pretty much there. The other day, the Mog scratched The Boy on the face and when I kissed it better, my lips swelled up in a way that the purveyors of collagen can still only dream about. Generally speaking, I have been avoiding sharp objects for fear of flying off into the horizon like a deflating balloon.

As a result of this, I have banned the cat. As a result of that, I have been called upon by four brown and pleading eyes to provide a substitute. It is a delicate subject. Obviously, I am against offering any animal a home on the grounds that I've recently discovered I don't particularly like them, but there is also the small matter of my own and my family's track record where domestic animals are concerned, which frankly doesn't inspire confidence.

I used to think that the high turnover of pets that passed through the Looney household was indicative of our great love and compassion for the four-legged, but lately I've come to the conclusion that it was more to do with a somewhat cavalier attitude towards their well-being. Of the four dogs that put in hard time with our family, two were dispatched to 'farms', one was given to a 'nice old couple' and the other one just vanished one day without any real explanation. In between, the local stray, a handsome boxer called Jasper, died in front of our house and when we queried the cause of death, we were assured that he had simply 'burst'. I've no idea what actually befell Jasper, but I do know that we commemorated his somewhat bizarre exit by christening the grapes in tins of fruit cocktail 'jaspers' and bursting them with spoons in a sort of solemn ceremony. To this day, no member of my family can see a tin of fruit cocktail without thinking of Jasper.

We also had a kitten that mysteriously never became a cat and a handful of rabbits, all called Bugs, who never troubled the longevity pages of the *Guinness Book of Records*. We did have one very old rabbit, but that was already a pensioner by the time we got it (from a 'nice old couple') and suffice to say that it didn't hang around to bother the bunny queen's telegram staff. We had goldfish that drowned and a bat that lived for about an hour and a half. Oh, and we had seventy-six guinea pigs.

Actually, the plague of pigs was mine, and was caused by my tearful protests when the initial pair started to breed and the words 'nice old couple' were again whispered. So I got to keep the litter and all the subsequent litters on the understanding that I would feed and clean them and that the buck would stop with me. Unfortunately he didn't, and by the time he'd impregnated his missus, all his daughters and most of his first cousins, they were so inbred and mad that within a short period of time they all (literally) keeled over and died. Before doing so, though, they provided me with years of enjoyment wrapped up in a pungent odour. I discovered, for example, that their little purrs of pleasure came in different tones and so I set up a sort of guinea pig choir, which functioned by being rubbed up the wrong way. I also learnt that physiologically, the guinea pig is the closest small animal to the human: on that, all I will say is that if you are an adult male, try not to let your bottom get completely clogged up with dirt or you'll risk an unstoppable erection which may trigger a heart attack.

After all that, my parents took on another cat which lived a long and utterly spoilt life, prolonged by kidney dialysis and its having its own bedroom. I, unfortunately, have made no such amends and so the current demands for animal company will have to go unmet. After all, as Uncle George might have said, better two pairs of disappointed brown eyes than seventy-six pairs of wild staring ones.

CHRISTMAS SORTED

SMALL GIRL: 4 YEARS, 5 MONTHS
BOY: 2 YEARS, 4 MONTHS

Since August, I have been boasting about how organised I'm going to be this Christmas. Not for me the last minute dash into town in search of something in a 16-and-a-half collar. I shall have my wrapping paper bought and dispatched long before it hits its five sheets for fifty final reduction. Christmas Eve will dawn with my turkey oven-ready, instead of a mere twinkle in the Superquinn butcher's eye. The scheduled arrival of the new baby – 'Mammy's Christmas present', as The Small Girl has generously coined it – in the week before the glorious day, means that everything has to be done, dusted and decked out way in advance of the usual deadline. If Auntie Maureen's lavender soap and body lotion set aren't bought and wrapped by 15 December, then Auntie Maureen will have to go without.

Luckily, I haven't got an Auntie Maureen, which is just as well since it's December, and predictably, I haven't a thing done. Not a present bought, not a sprout sized up, not a child in the house washed. It's probably fair to say that the Taliban are better prepared for this Christmas than I am.

Of course, it would have helped if I'd had some co-operation in executing my seasonally adjusted plans – but somehow, people just don't attach the same urgency to the old 'what do you want for Christmas' request when it's posed in September as they do when it's made from a pub pay phone on Christmas Eve. In short, everybody still has to get back to me – a situation which may imminently result in, horror of horror, my having to use my initiative. On the plus side, my family is peculiarly lacking in both imagination and expectation where Christmas gifts are concerned, and so, in a curious dress rehearsal for the euro changeover, the common currency amongst the Looneys has, for some Christmases past, been Woodies' vouchers.

This ceremonial mass exchange of vouchers come Christmas Day means that nobody's disappointed (bar the five-sheets-of-wrapping-paper-for-fifty brigade) and provided nobody's gone mad (given a €30 token and received a €20), a serene sense of equality prevails throughout the land. The vouchers I can manage to buy (though I haven't); it is the more immediate kin and friends who are presenting all manner of problems. The Husband, for example, is less likely to be impressed by DIY vouchers than some other close relatives (this in spite of the fact that he, as an official Handy-Round-The-House sort, is the sole benefactor of them). I think he believes that it is enough that he must paint the entire house himself without accepting the paint as a gift where he might stand to gain, for example, a DVD player. My point – that confinement waits for no man and that if he doesn't make his mind up soon he'll get neither – doesn't appear to carry nearly as much weight as I do.

But it is the children who are really slowing things up, festive-wise. As he is similarly occupied in the days before Christmas Eve, Santa Claus made it clear to me some time ago that he needs to check this household's list twice as soon as possible, but thus far, there's been no white smoke to carry any note up our chimney. The Boy is young enough and male enough to have become singularly obsessed with Buzz Lightyear, and so can be easily accommodated (though again, of course, he hasn't been), but The Small Girl, the advertising industry's young dream, cannot make up her mind for love nor money. Every ad break on television brings with it a new delight and a new conviction that this is the present for her, and each night's sleep effectively wipes her memory of all traces of the toy, its delights, and any notion that it might have enriched her life. We start each new day with a clean slate and an empty shopping list, only to have it quickly filled with the last item from each ad break. Thus, in a single day, we can get through a wish list of Baby Wee Wee (who has a plastic scrotum and as such is unwelcome in our home), Robot Baby, Digimon Gameboy and Persil Non-Bio. My fingers may be crossed that she will finally settle on the latter, but I fear that she will simply continue to procrastinate till the New Year. I hope she likes Woodies' vouchers.

All of this is by way of announcing that since I've a metaphorical bun to remove from the oven before the turkey goes in, I'm taking a break for a while. Until then, may I take this (premature) opportunity to wish you all a merry Christmas and a prosperous New Year. And while I'm at it, a glorious St Patrick's Day and a Happy Easter as well. There, I feel better organised already.

AND THEN THERE WERE THREE

SMALL GIRL: 4 YEARS, 10 MONTHS
BOY: 2 YEARS, 9 MONTHS
BABY: 4 MONTHS

As The Boy is fond of announcing when he re-enters a room, I back. My absence was caused by the arrival, just a couple of days before Christmas, of an almost implausibly gorgeous little girl; my return is precipitated by my failure, between times, to win the lottery (and, of course, because I missed the buzz of publishing. But mainly the lottery thing).

The Baby, since you ask, is a rhapsody in pink. Having produced two of the least obliging infants in modern obstetrics, we had reached the conclusion that babies who slept and smiled and seemed generally glad to be here, were put upon this earth to torment us. But now we've suddenly been blessed with one of our very own; the kind of child who always appears to be in the presence of an apparition for one. Either that, or she's every bit as bad as the first two and our standards have slipped so far that we can no longer tell the difference.

But even independent witnesses will testify to the pure goodness of this latest financial drain. She is, as one of my fellow inmates in the Coombe hospital observed, 'a fucking angel'. This same new mother later addressed a vol-au-vent with a rallying cry of 'what the FUCK is this?', but in matters of small children she counted herself as something of an expert, having had so many that she had considered 'asking them to fuckin' sew it up while they were at it.'

Ah yes, the Coombe. I mention it only because we're facing into an election and those of you lucky enough not to have had babies in the public health sector in the past couple of years should know how utterly and chronically under-funded and under-staffed our maternity services are. And while I have a whole evening's worth of amusing anecdotes from the experience (most of them at the expense of the teenage mothers, heroin addicts and other afflicted women with whom I shared a ward), the reality of it wasn't even remotely funny. All I can do is pay tribute to the staff, Herculean in the face of adversity, and slag off the government which has allowed the whole maternity sector to decline to the point where it is an actual health hazard. Trust me, I'm not a doctor, but I do know that unless the problem is addressed soon, women and babies are going to die, and I can only give thanks that the angel and I limped away from the experience with nothing more serious than culture shock.

Anyway, the whole hospital business was so traumatic that we neglected to give the child a name for the first few days – something that prompted the very strange woman in the bed opposite mine to nominate, every ninety seconds or so, a different name for my consideration. As far as I could ascertain, these names were absolutely random and arbitrary and were predictable only in their regularity. 'Rachel!', she would shout one minute, and I would pretend to consider it. Then, while I thought we were still on Rachel, she'd shout 'Cheryl!' and we'd begin the charade again. This wouldn't have been too unpleasant if it hadn't gone on for *hours* at a time, and if it hadn't been accompanied by a certain degree of menace. But it did and it was, and by the time she was discharged I was reduced to reading only broadsheet newspapers in order to avoid eye contact.

In the end we chose something Irish and unpronounceable

which we pretty much made up ourselves. It means 'Little Lamb' ('fucking angel' didn't really translate) which suits her perfectly, and when she's twenty and struggling with a weight problem, I trust she'll remember to thank us for it.

Of course, lest you think our life a Moses basket of roses, the older two have continued to doggedly plough their furrow of bad behaviour in the presence of their new sister. The Small Girl is in favour of The Baby in principle but has taken to eating her own clothes in what may be a subliminal protest, while The Boy – though surprisingly gentle and loving with his usurper – went completely mental for a couple of months and has now settled back into his old, petulant lifestyle, with the addition of a taste for public urination and an enthusiastic interest in his own newly-discovered genitals. We couldn't be more proud.

In fact, on the occasion that we got out together (who says you can't have a social life with three children under five?) we reflected that while the eldest two have ground us down, worn us out and generally disappointed us at every turn, the new baby is a pure joy. Oh, but give her time.

DROMO-LAND

SMALL GIRL: 4 YEARS, 11 MONTHS
BOY: 2 YEARS, 10 MONTHS
BABY: 5 MONTHS

I sometimes think that if I could learn to pass a bargain then I wouldn't spend so much of my time surrounded by people with tattoos. But every time I try to better myself, I fall at the last fence, tick the box marked 'Economy' and end up wondering where all the posh people are.

Most other women, for example, might reward themselves for having expanded their family by persuading their admiring husband to whisk them away for a short, romantic break *à deux* in, say, Dromoland Castle, while doting if addled grandparents mind the new improved family back home. But most other women's heads aren't turned by promotional offers on tins of Bachelor's beans. Most other women probably don't ease the labels off the tins, pore over the tiny print and then send the coupon off to Bachelor's so that they might be sent a big fat voucher for a discount weekend *for the whole family.* Let's face it, when most people say they're going to Dromoland, they mean the Castle. Not us. Our trip to Dromoland was to the Bachelor's Beans promotion at the Clare Inn Hotel, right beside it. Not really Dromoland, as The Husband put it. More Dromo-Land.

Still, it might have been Disney Land as far as the under-fives were concerned. The great advantage of very young children is that you can sell them any old pig in a poke and call it quality ham. It has only recently dawned on The Boy, for example, that the toy he's been calling Bob The Builder for the past year is, in fact, a truck driver called Bill. Likewise, while most older children would have some kind of mental breakdown at the prospect of a home-made Mickey Mouse, The Small Girl readily accepted the pensioner's version of the animated favourite, complete with his purple paisley waistcoat. No doubt they will become more discerning as they grow older; in the meantime, we are happy to exploit their innocence with bargain basement merchandise.

As it turned out, though, the Clare Inn was bargain basement only in price. In fact, if I couldn't have gone to Dromoland (and I couldn't), then Dromo-Land proved a perfectly agreeable substitute. From their apparent desire to take all three of the children away from us and keep them happy while we ate their big dinners and drank their big beers, to the basket of fruit that greeted us on our arrival, they actually put together a commendable package that any couple on the verge of family arbitration would have been glad of.

We swam in the pool, sang in the car, danced in the bar and spilt Coke pretty much everywhere. We even got to take the ferry over to visit Ballybunion, scene of my childhood holidays, on the kind of cloudless day that made me wonder why I ever stopped going.

I stopped going, of course, because at sixteen I entered the joyous time of life when people have no need of family discounts, early bird specials or children's menus. Now I've gone full circle and am doomed to wander the Earth – or at least the coastal regions of it – trying to find Things To Do With The Children That Don't Involve Television. Don't get me wrong – the Bachelor's Beans weekend at Dromo-Land was fine, but if we hadn't had three small children, we'd rather have had our toenails extracted on a pool table by nude GAA players than spend even five minutes there. It was absolutely heaving with harassed parents and sugar-high children and – perhaps because of the price tag – had clearly also attracted a number of people who'd never stayed in a hotel before. Hence we had the crowd who set off the fire alarm at five in the morning and the bewildered eejit who rang our room at 4am to talk dirty, if slightly incoherently, to me on the hotel phone. And all the time, just a scant mile away in the Castle, people were feasting on swans (I presume).

When we checked out, the receptionist presented me with a bill stamped 'Kia-Ora promotion'. I pointed out to her that we were, in fact, the Bachelor's Beans party and she shrugged and told me it didn't matter. Insofar as if you choose your holidays by peeling labels off jars then the name on the jar scarcely matters, she was quite right.

Before we left we went for a walk down to the lake behind the hotel and out of the evening mist, we saw Dromoland Castle in the distance, as though suspended on a cloud. For a moment, I thought it laughed at us. 'That's a fairytale castle,' said The Small Girl. Then we turned, got into our 93 D pumpkin and headed for home.

YELLOW SUBMARINERS

SMALL GIRL: 5 YEARS
BOY: 2 YEARS, 11 MONTHS
BABY: 6 MONTHS

There is no easy way to say this: my almost three-year-old son thinks he is John Lennon.

It started innocently enough – a toddler picking up snatches of Beatles' songs from a tape in the car. Singing along a bit, getting the words wrong in a cutesy kind of way, nothing untoward. Then requesting the tape himself, and a CD as well, featuring different tracks. Still within the spectrum of cute, though; we even video-taped him singing along to 'She Loves You'.

But then it started to get serious. He is forbidden from entering our home office, but it drew him like a Beatles-sounding siren. Because there, all along the bottom shelf, is the hard stuff – the vinyl. All the original recordings, all lovingly preserved. And suddenly, the requests started getting more specific. Revolver, side one. The Yellow Submarine soundtrack, side two. Inevitably, the videos followed. *Magical Mystery Tour. Yellow Submarine.* The Beatles Anthology (get this) – part seven

Just before Christmas, I began to suspect that the situation was no longer something Penelope Leach could sort out. We were in the doctor's crowded waiting room for an ante-natal check-up and The Boy took his sister's hands, invited her to dance and then sang 'Eleanor Rigby' to her as they slowly waltzed around the room. It was the frightened look in the other patients' eyes that alerted me to the fact that we were now way, way past cute.

Since then, to be brief, he has become so obsessed with The Beatles in general and 'Yellow Submarine' in particular that he requests the video all day, every day and gets it, I must admit, about three times a week. As soon as it ends he bursts into tears and tells us he 'misses Yellow Submarine'. The Husband, who is handy enough in the art department, has drawn an outline of a yellow submarine and photocopied it so that The Boy always has a yellow submarine to colour in when he needs one, which is pretty much most of the time. When we finally get around to decorating his room, we've agreed that we will paint a yellow submarine on the wall. And for the last two weeks, he has invited us to call him John. Last weekend, he threw a strop in a café, and moved to a table on his own where he sat with his arms crossed singing 'Nowhere Man' and addressing me as Ringo.

I blame The Husband, of course. He is the worst kind of Beatles fan – one who comes from Liverpool. And while he protests that none of this is his fault and that he never tried to indoctrinate the children, they didn't lick The Beatles off the stones and they certainly didn't get it from me. Now, I don't have a problem with the Fab Four per se; I would just like my children to appreciate music that is a little more, well, contemporary. On this front, The Small Girl has delivered – while she's not averse to a spot of 'I Don't Care Too Much For Money', she appreciates that money can buy you S Club 7 records and is the better for it.

I realise that I've painted The Boy as utterly mad, but I honestly believe that his obsession has more to do with boys generally than

The Beatles in particular. Before John Lennon there was Buzz Lightyear, and if the *Toy Story* obsession didn't run quite so deep as his current passion, then it's probably only because The Husband didn't have a tantalising hoard of Buzz memorabilia stashed in his wardrobe (at least, I hope he didn't).

But it is a fact that boys get far more involved with their hobbies than girls. I remember my own brother getting into dinosaurs and learning the names and dietary requirements of every one while I just skimmed the surface of my girlie hobbies. I briefly liked birds, for example, but the sum total of my obsession ran to an awareness that humming birds were the smallest of all and that there was something peculiar about kingfishers, though I can't now remember what it was. But I'll bet my big brother could still feed a triceratops.

It could be argued (and usually is) that women have better things to worry about. I would certainly hope that as The Boy's world expands, his interest in yellow submarines will sink to the bottom of the sea of his knowledge and that by the time he's grown up, he will no longer think of The Beatles as his entire *raison d'être* and, more specifically, of his mother as Ringo Starr. In the meantime, The Husband's love of The Beatles has taken a whole new and novel direction. I sense we are at the beginning of a long and winding road.

WEDDING ANNIVERSARY

SMALL GIRL: 5 YEAR, 3 MONTHS
BOY: 3 YEARS, 2 MONTHS
BABY: 9 MONTHS

If there is one thing The Husband and I are completely in agreement on, it's that our wedding day was the best day of our lives. So quite why the anniversary of that perfect day is traditionally the worst day of the year for us is a bit of a mystery. It is as though somebody up there knows that the 21st of September can never be as good for us again, and decides to make an absolute hames of it in order that it won't pale by comparison.

Our first wedding anniversary set the standard by which all subsequent ones have been measured. It happened to coincide (as it always does) with the wedding anniversary of my best friend, whose lovely husband phoned me up in London and solicited my help in organising a fabulous surprise weekend away in the Smoke for their big day. Flights were booked, a hotel was found, a Conran restaurant was reserved – and as an added bonus, I arranged for a bottle of champagne and flowers to be in their room when they arrived. It was their seventh anniversary and they had a lovely time. It was our first, and we spent it in KFC. Him, me, The Baby and (get this) his entire family, who had a full-scale row over their Tower burgers while I pushed the buggy back and forward trying to get The Small Girl – who in retrospect was mental – to stop crying.

Oh, oh, I almost forgot. While the happy couple were waking up to Buck's Fizz and room service, I awoke on the morning of the anniversary to be greeted by my mother-in-law, who was staying with us (oh yes), and cheerfully told me that 'Steve (The Husband) did get you a card, but he's lost it.'

Frankly, that we got to a second anniversary was a shade short of miraculous. But we did, and so too did the mother-in-law, who again chose to mark the happy day in our home. I think that was the year that she shared our Chinese takeaway and then gave out shite to me for ordering a dish with green peppers in it, when she hates green peppers. There were no such culinary disasters the following year, when we were at her place and she cooked us a special celebratory meal of tinned ham and chips. We even had a nip of dessert wine. Three years and two children, we all mused. Could we *be* any happier?

If it sounds as though I'm blaming the unfortunate mother-in-law for all this, then let me clarify the matter. It wasn't her fault at all, it was wholly The Husband's. By year four I'd decided I knew him well enough to tell him I didn't want to spend our wedding anniversary with his mother any more and by year five, I'd plucked up the courage to tell him I no longer wanted petrol-station carnations with which to mark the occasion.

Which bring us, tidily, to year six. In fairness, this time he really tried. Unbeknownst to me, the plan, a month ago, was for us to eat in our favourite restaurant, The Tea Room, and then spend the night in the Clarence. Then the hitherto beautifully behaved Baby decided that whatever about the anniversary, the honeymoon was certainly over. Almost simultaneously, she gave up sleep and liking people and with it, we gave up any notion of spending a night away from her. But we'd always have The Tea Room, we thought, so I went out and bought a fabulous new outfit and high heels so sharp I could have skewered a green pepper on them. I even wore jewellery in my belly button. It became apparent that the staff of The Tea Room were to be deprived of my vision of loveliness around tea-time, when The Baby failed to respond to the antibiotics and enthusiastically vomited all over me, the sofa, the floor and herself. In the ensuing clean-up operation, she managed to stab The Husband up the nose with a tiny fingernail and his subsequent violent nosebleed made the pool of sick look half-baked. In the middle of it all, The Boy, who has gone a bit mad, wandered in and – not unreasonably – asked 'can I sleep in your bed with my teddy … in my nude?' I tried to think what it all might mean but the only clear answer was that it meant we were going nowhere. We cancelled everything but The Babysitter, who agreed to come anyway just in case anyone went to sleep. In the end, at 10 o'clock, we teetered into our local for two bottles of beer. Overdressed and undernourished, we then picked up a Chinese takeaway and were home for eleven. As we decided to leave the champagne unopened, we agreed on one more thing. It had been our best anniversary ever. Then we went to bed. Just the three of us.

ALL THE FUN OF THE FAIR

SMALL GIRL: 5 YEARS, 4 MONTHS
BOY: 3 YEARS, 3 MONTHS
BABY: 10 MONTHS

All three of my children have a small red mark between their eyebrows. As far as I can see, that's been my only contribution to their genetic make-up.

Oh, people try to put them down to me – but noting that The Small Girl's hair is cut in a vaguely similar style to my own is hardly confirmation of a miniature doppelgänger. Others just stare into the three little faces in the hope that something – a nose, a mouth – will ring a bell, but nothing ever does. Even my own parents, convinced that they must take after our side of the family, can only muster up a passing resemblance in one of the kids to one of my sisters. The awful truth is out there: while none of them is a ringer for their dad, they all physically favour him over me. Where genes are concerned, I am Falmer's to his Levi's.

Even leaving the looks issue to one side, they're all his. The Small Girl has demonstrated a proportional musical talent and so has been dispatched to the College of Music to have it honed. Although I'm the one who brings her to Chatham Row, waits for her, brings her home again and makes her mad instruments for her class, strictly speaking, her music has nothing to do with me. She's also reasonably useful with a packet of markers – again, her father's daughter. Show her a clutch of words, meanwhile – and while I, at five, would have craved to learn them all and more – she glazes over, announces she's 'fed up' and heads for 'The Hills Are Alive'.

Only in one area of her life can I recognise myself. Like her mother, she is physically timid. She's unlikely to be troubling the *Guinness Book of Records* with any feats of sporting or physical magnificence. In the swimming pool she hogs the bar and even in the everyday kids' stuff of playgrounds, swings and slides, she keeps her feet firmly on the ground. In other words, she's no fun at a fair.

This was underlined a couple of weeks back when we took in a fair somewhere on the dark side of the M50. While the perpetually surly carnival workers were content to take a fortune off The Boy, who wanted to go on everything that was nailed down (and probably quite a few things that weren't), The Small Girl stared in horror at everything from the Gently Rotating Teacups to the Slooooower Than This Choo-Choo. The narky part of me, inevitably, kept trying to force her to go on things, but my inner self recognised all too well the quivering child terrified by anything faster than a cycle path.

Just for a moment I was back at Funderland, watching the rest of the world having a ball and wondering why, for me, the big rides were always out of the question. In fact, the closest I came to a white-knuckle experience back then was when I was about ten and a filthy old man pressed himself against me and felt my bum at the Hook-A-Duck stall. It was a bewildering encounter and the only mercy was that the man didn't charge me for it. Would that the sullen carnival workers had adopted the same philanthropic approach. As it was, ride or no ride, Funderland used to be the easiest way to blow your pocket-money and have nothing to show for it but a quick puke on the 18 bus back home.

Still, it's reassuring to note that, all these years later, fun fairs still have an aphrodisiac effect on some. At the one we went to – let's call it Skangerland – we were treated to the sight of an endless stream of young teenage couples wearing the faces off each other with a fervour that bordered on violence. It's funny, I can remember being those teenagers and thinking adults were scandalised by our energetic public snogging – now I know that they were just laughing up their sleeves at us. That said, I can honestly say I never wore the face off anyone for twenty-five minutes outside a curry chips concession called 'A Touch of Class' in a field at a fair.

Anyway, eventually I forced my first born to go on the Gently Rotating Teacups and – as I knew she would be – she was the better for it. On the way home she asked if we could go again the next day and we assured her that we could not. Life may be a roller coaster – as Ronan Keating has claimed – but you've got to take these things in baby steps. Next time, we might even chance the curry chips: after all, if you are planning on defying death, you might as well do it with a touch of class.

AN UNFORTUNATE EVENT

SMALL GIRL: 5 YEARS, 4 MONTHS
BOY: 3 YEARS, 3 MONTHS
BABY: 10 MONTHS

When bad things happen to good people, they invariably discover that everyone else's cousin has had it much worse. As you will recall if you've been paying attention, I first became acquainted with this principle when The Small Girl was born, eight weeks early and tipping the scales at just three pounds and ten ounces. All of a sudden I was inundated with unlikely stories of tiny morsels, unscheduled babies weighing just a pound who – without exception – finished up as burly six footers. Everyone's cousin had had a premature baby; every next-door neighbour knew someone who knew someone who was so small their father could hold them in the palm of his hand. Thus was our trauma undermined with kind words. By the time The Small Girl left hospital, three weeks later, we'd documented so many Pound Babies that we wondered why they bothered making regular sized babygros at all.

Unfortunately, we've now witnessed a second application of the Cousin Rule. A couple of weeks ago, a truly horrendous accident at the swimming pool left The Boy – the previously perfect Boy – without one of his front teeth. Even as I was scrambling around for the newly liberated gnasher and mopping what seemed like gallons of blood from his poor screaming mouth, toothless cousins throughout south Dublin were being mustered for my consideration. *Exactly* the same thing had happened to so many people, I was informed, and all of them were just grand, and toothy as you like. I even heard of one who'd grown a third tooth, after his baby and permanent teeth both made sudden and violent departures. And inevitably, as the days went on and The Boy's smile returned – albeit now with a gap you could drive the Luas through – the lot of the cousins and neighbours got ever more acute. There was the girl who was run over outside her house (nothing to do with her teeth, but held up as an example of how it could have been much worse) and the boy who broke all his front teeth and then lost one of his permanent ones on a rugby field. There were children with cancer, adults with dentures and afflictions at all points in between. The moral, to borrow from The Beautiful South, is that if you've been far, there's always someone who's been further than your far. Of course, it was all meant to make us feel much better, but inevitably, it just came across to my bruised psyche as a huge wave of (rightful) scorn of my obsession with the aesthetic.

Yet even in a serious crisis, application of the Cousin Rule doesn't always have the desired effect. I remember, some years ago, going to visit a friend in hospital on the eve of a serious back operation – a last desperate attempt to correct an acute and incredibly rare condition. As she lay on her stomach, wincing in pain, she told me that in spite of her doctors' pessimism, she would be just fine because 'apparently, everyone in The Pines has had this operation.' Her brother, a frequenter of the aforementioned hostelry, had applied the Cousin Rule in spades to ease her mind and had succeeded only in worrying her more and giving her concern about his own drinking habits. In the end, she made a good recovery – though needless to say, not as good as everyone in The Pines and the horses they rode in on.

But back to the horrendous accident. I blame the pool architects, for configuring the seating area in the way they did, The Husband, for being away for the weekend and forcing me to take all three children to The Small Girl's swimming lesson, The Boy, for being a boy, John Major, for having an affair with Edwina Currie and obliging me to gossip about it with the woman next to me, but chiefly I blame myself. Above all, I'm beating myself up for being so shallow that I quietly would have preferred if my previously perfect son had broken an arm instead of losing a tooth.

The only consolation is that the whole sorry affair has brought me a sort of local celebrity. As schedulers have recently learnt, all the radio and television appearances in the world can't compete with real-life drama, and suddenly, strangers are stopping me in the shops to ask after The Boy and regale me with toothless tales of their own. I have become The Mother of The Boy Who Had The Accident At The Swimming Pool, an unfortunate to join the ranks of the other local unfortunates. I have been blooded, literally and figuratively, and every other mother wants to shake my trembling hand in the Uncle Ben's aisle. And, of course, to introduce me to their imperfect cousin.

... ACTUALLY, A SERIES OF UNFORTUNATE EVENTS

SMALL GIRL: 5 YEARS, 5 MONTHS
BOY: 3 YEARS, 4 MONTHS
BABY: 11 MONTHS

Of all the advice I was given when I was expecting our first child, the most bizarre came from a retired mother and ran as follows: when you're taking your injured child and subsequent damaged offspring to casualty, always give a false name and address. By doing this, the authorities won't notice how frequent your visits actually are and they'll be unable to take your kids into care.

While I never followed it to the letter, I feel my short years at the helm of three children have equipped me to modify this advice somewhat and pass it on to others who may be in the first hot flush of childbirth: to wit, always try to ensure that your children's serious accidents occur in different countries. On the presumption that the authorities in other jurisdictions don't routinely compare notes, they won't notice how frequent your visits actually are and they'll be unable to take your kids into care.

For example, when The Husband almost broke The Small Girl's arm during some particularly emphatic horseplay, we were quite happy to give Tallaght Hospital our real names on the basis that prior to that unfortunate incident they'd never heard of us. They couldn't have known about the infant Boy's meningitis scare for the simple reason that it had happened in the Canary Islands, and had been resolutely ignored by the only English-speaking doctor in the area on the basis that it coincided with his siesta. Likewise, they couldn't have taken The Small Girl's previous torn ligaments into consideration because again, they happened outside their manor, this time in a playground in France.

Well, the good news this week is that our Irish medical record remains virtually unblemished, while yet another country is picking up the tab for our injured offspring. The latest lucky winner is England, and the city of Liverpool and Arrowe Park Hospital in particular. The whole sorry business happened last weekend during our visit to the mother-in-law – a now annual pilgrimage we take in order to throw all the out-of-date food out of her fridge. It's a tough job but to The Husband, it's more of a hobby.

Anyway, we were on the home straight when (relative) tragedy struck. As both her siblings have before her, The Baby inserted her finger into the hinge of the bathroom door. But uniquely, as she did so, The Boy kicked the door closed, causing the ten-month-old little finger to effectively burst. In the first sixty seconds after the accident, the following happened: I ran the finger under the cold tap, phoned The Husband to get him back from the pub, breast-fed the screaming child, put my boots on, found out where the nearest casualty department was and had a surreal conversation with the mother-in-law about which jacket I wanted to wear. The Baby, meanwhile, lost more blood than I would have believed a small body like hers contained. Most of it, inevitably, was absorbed by my top, which, equally inevitably, was white.

Now as it turned out, this was a fortuitous choice of outfit. By the time I ran through the door of Arrowe Park accident and emergency department, I resembled nothing less than a miniature Battle of the Somme. My face and arms were blood-spattered, my white top no longer worthy of the description and The Baby, by now asleep, looked for all the world like a Bennetton ad. The net result of all this cosmetic carnage was that we were rushed through the waiting room and straight into a waiting cubicle before the hundred odd half-people who'd queued for hours could say 'Jack Robinson's stabbed me and I've only minutes to live.' 'It looks a lot worse than it is,' I meekly informed the medics who swarmed around us like a petrol-blue SWAT team, 'She's just cut her finger.' They weren't to be put off by such protests, however, and a dozen or so of them got to work on the tiny, bloody digit, while another barked at a nurse who was mopping up vomit to 'spray more gel, I can still smell the alcohol in here.' I hadn't the nerve to tell them that it was probably me.

We were done in minutes, X-ray and all, and coughed back out onto the streets of Liverpool before the authorities in Dublin even noticed we were gone. On the way back to Hell's Fridge, we reflected on the fact that – amazingly – the only one of our children who hasn't now put in time in casualty is The Boy. This is in spite of the fact that he has suffered the most horrific accidents of all of them, and has the scar and the gap in his mouth to prove it. I mention this, of course, with fingers and legs crossed, all the wood at my disposal in my grasp and an aspiration to the Sacred Heart on my tongue. If we can also avoid leaving the country again till he's over twenty-one, we might just get away with it.

I'M DREAMING ...

SMALL GIRL: 5 YEARS, 6 MONTHS
BOY: 3 YEARS, 5 MONTHS
BABY: 11 MONTHS

I have two very distinct memories of visits to Santa Claus from my childhood. The first happened in Dunnes Stores in Cornelscourt on the cusp of the 1970s, and featured yours truly, an unusually square-shaped pre-schooler and my bestest buddy, Gary Rogers from across the road. In a nutshell, while I was more than happy to take Santa by the hand – with barely an introduction – and sally forth into the depths of his grotto for a frank exchange of views, Gary, the boy, cried for Ireland and refused to have anything to do with the whole business. It was an example of Girl Power at a time before most of the Spice Girls were born and Geri Halliwell was still in long pants.

My other vivid grotto experience dates from the other end of the Santa spectrum and happened in Penneys in Rathfarnham. Sitting in a pisspoor surround that, as far as I can recall, was just the passport photo machine with a red curtain around it, the World's Worst Santa greeted this eight-year-old with the words, 'Aren't you a bit old for this?' If I wasn't on the way in, then I sure as hell was on the way out. My wonder years were over, courtesy of a disaffected seasonal worker on an adjustable stool.

I had a third, slightly more surreal Santa encounter a few years back when I was dispatched, as a cub reporter, to write an article about Santa's first outing in the then spanking new Square in Tallaght. This particular man in red sticks in my memory for two reasons: not only was he younger than me, but he had one of those wispy moustaches and the accompanying skin condition that were terribly popular in Dublin southwest at the time. I had reason to visit the selfsame shopping centre recently (we go there from time to time to be smoked at) and was pleased to note that their festive representative this year is above voting age. I was equally pleased to note that somebody has placed two fibreglass polar bears in an obviously sexually provocative position, known colloquially as 'doggy style'.

Of course, my own children are too young to appreciate such subtleties, but they're old enough to do a Gary Rogers, and so we're anxious that their Santa encounters be entirely positive ones. To this end, we whistled away two-and-a-half hours last Christmas queuing in Arnott's to see The World's Best Santa. Unfortunately, he was a bit too good for The Boy, who had to be carried in and practically airlifted out, along with his eight-and-a-half-months pregnant mother. In between times, he buried his head in my shoulder while The Small Girl happily posed for photos and explained the principle of the Kitten-In-A-Box that she was hankering after for the Big Day.

But these things stay with them. The World's Best Santa brings his own beard to work, unlike the interloper we chewed the fat with in Santa's Kingdom in Punchestown this week. Since The Boy is currently waking up every morning in tears because Santa hasn't come, we'd taken the precaution of not telling them in advance where our 'adventure' was leading us. It wasn't until we were inside the massive hangar and engaging with a youth in a foolish hat that the cent dropped with either of them that here be Christmas fare. Two hours later, having marvelled at a mocked-up space shuttle, wandered a North Pole village street, waved at Santa's missus and admired a cluster of sorry-looking reindeer, they were ready for the finale. But however magical the experience (and from a grown up's perspective, it's only barely so and could do with a whole heap of soundproofing) and in spite of the collective pretence, we were still in Ireland. So, inevitably, it had to finish with an Irish man behind a cotton-wool beard talking too much. In fact, so obliging was this particular Santa that we had to end the interview ourselves, explaining with some embarrassment that we had to get on. In any case, while Santa seemed happy to shoot the breeze for hours – 'Now, how about a photo with *all* of you in it?' –

and The Boy was making up for last year's performance by practically mating with the unfortunate man's leg, The Small Girl was staring at him in a most suspicious manner. Beyond a whispered 'Barbie Karaoke Machine', she was noticeably unwilling to discuss chimney cleaning methods or carrots for reindeers with the man of the moment. In the end, quite literally, we made our excuses and left. On the way home, The Small Girl announced with a degree of certainty that that wasn't the real Santa and The Boy battered her because he knew for sure it was. Only seventeen days to go, God help us all.

THE PARTY SEASON

SMALL GIRL: 5 YEARS, 6 MONTHS
BOY: 3 YEARS, 5 MONTHS
BABY: 11 MONTHS

You can tell it's really close now because when people ask 'All set for Christmas?', they no longer laugh in an ironic way afterwards. Unfortunately, irony or no irony, the answer remains the same: not by a turkey's neck. I would like to be able to claim that I have managed to order the turkey and ham and possibly sent a couple of cards. But the current reality is that this time last year I was lying very still in the Coombe Hospital contemplating a Caesarean scar and a new financial dependent, and I was still infinitely better prepared for Christmas than I am now.

In between times I have become the most popular party girl on the block, and therein lies the rub. It's relatively easy to arrange Christmas when you're nine months pregnant because by and (especially) large, people let you get on with it in the presumption that there really isn't anything else you'd rather be doing. But lose the weight, acquire a pair of fuck-me boots and threaten to pierce your belly button and suddenly everyone wants you to party on down. So while last year's festive calendar involved two declined invitations, this year's has seen compulsory attendance at five top-grade bashes, two refusals and the promise of a significant amount of booty shaking in the days to come. Apparently, I'm suddenly great craic.

Some of these parties have even involved adults, but for the most part, they have been all about The Small Girl prancing around in a variety of seasonally adjusted outfits in front of an audience of approving mothers and video-camera toting fathers. I'm aware that I've got off relatively lightly on this front, since the two younger children are still at the invited-audience only stage. Every day this week, I have met my peers rushing between tin whistle recitals, productions of *Annie* and *Oliver*, festive gymnastic displays, carol services, prayer services and rehearsals for all of the above – and I have projected ahead with a certain sense of dread to the time when my Christmas social commitments will be multiplied by three. If my current festive-preparation rate is anything to measure, by then I'll have to start cooking in June.

But even the best-laid plans can only be executed in full in the days immediately preceding Christmas Day. There would have been little point, for example, in my getting my hair done for Christmas back in September – but now I find that, in effect, I did, since I literally cannot find two hours to spare between now and then in which to get my roots resprayed. The Small Girl also needs a trip to the hairdressers, but again, her whirl of speech and drama and music-related performances preclude her from making that appointment.

So that explains the entry 'hair x 2' on the note that is currently stuck to our fridge. The same list, you might be frightened to learn, also includes the following: 'Clean car, put up curtains, assemble shelves, paint hall radiator, put up light fittings, clean out spare bedroom'. I haven't included buy presents and food, cook up a storm, wrap presents, receive and be grateful for the mother- and-brother-in-law and maintain at all times a cheery disposition, because they all come under the heading of The Bleeding Obvious and don't need to be mentioned on the fridge.

Now all of that might sound as though this Christmas business is more trouble than it's worth round these parts, but since we are now a mere caught breath away from it, let me assure you that for all its chaotic surroundings, I adore this time of year. I love the giddiness, the quality television (though these years, I hardly seem to see anything of it), the Phil Spector album, the good food, the plentiful drink, the men in their good clothes, the children destroying their new clothes and the sense that everyone is erring on the side of bonhomie. I hold the distinction of probably being the youngest person ever to be described as 'cynical' on a school report, but for one week only I suspend all scoffing and scepticism in favour of a positively idiotic disposition. Above all, I love the Santa thing, which I can honestly say I get more from now than I did when I was a trembling child. The trouble back then was that there were no guarantees, whereas now – for the grown-ups at least – there are no surprises, and you know exactly which little face to watch at every precious second.

'Oh, I wish it could be Christmas every day', Wizard once sang. On days like these, I sometimes think they had the right idea. Then I look in the mirror and realise what colour my hair would be if that really were the case. All considered, once a year is probably about all the magic I can handle.

NEW YEAR'S RESOLUTIONS

SMALL GIRL: 5 YEARS, 7 MONTHS
BOY: 3 YEARS, 6 MONTHS
BABY: 1 YEAR, 1 MONTH

Less than a fortnight in, and already the New Year's resolutions are showing a certain lack of, well, resolve. The grown-ups in our house had sworn not to swear in front of the children, but a combination of cold weather, school holidays and close proximity to the aforementioned impressionables has meant that the air was already turning a vague shade of turquoise just a few days into 2003. By now, it has a distinctly cobalt hue. I, at least, have made some effort; as far as I can ascertain The Husband's only concession on this point has been to snigger quietly every time he 'f's or blinds. The only consolation for me is that it will be his mother who disinherits us when The Boy starts fecking her out of it, and not mine.

The little people have scarcely fared better. The Boy, who readily agreed to the whole New Leaf business, announced on New Year's Eve that his contribution to the world in 2003 would be to 'drink milk' – something that he energetically spent most of 2002 avoiding. This seemed like a great idea to his Unfortunate Mother, who duly served up a tall cold one the following day. 'Delicious!' came the affirming cry as the first mouthful disappeared, whereupon he pushed it away and demanded a glass of water. But you said you'd drink milk, protested the UM. 'And I just did,' he happily confirmed.

The Small Girl, meanwhile, who cannot use a knife and fork, close her coat, dress herself in anything other than a comical fashion or wipe her own bottom, gave the whole resolutions business a great deal of thought and eventually announced that she would 'get better at drawing'. It was, perhaps, a realistic self-assessment – and in fairness to her, it was far more achievable than her parents' lofty notions of getting through the day without calling a spade a fucking tool.

There was a time when I made New Year's resolutions about whole lifestyle changes; now I understand that a change is as good as a rest, and neither is in any way attainable at this point in my short life. So now I undertake modest promises, like the one I've made to myself to stop using the phrase 'as long as I'm alive' when dealing with the under five-and-a-halves.

My hand has been forced in this somewhat by The Boy's announcing to the woman stacking the shelves in Costcutters that in spite of the long minutes he spends gazing at the display, he will never have Coco Pops 'while my Mammy is still alive'. It is true that I have a flawed relationship with the Pops – and with chocolate-coated cereals in general – but to hear a three-year-old marking time until he can dance on my grave with a large bowl of snap, crackle and coco pop is a little depressing. It's clear I need to moderate my language in more ways than one.

(For all that, I do generally consider Coco Pops and their perfidious ilk to be the food of the devil, a breakfast time abomination that preys on the stupidity of children and the weariness of parents alike. As in all homes, the lofty idealism that I preached before I had children has gradually been eroded by their pestering and my exhaustion, so that in our house, there are more videos watched and more sweets eaten that I would like – but I will never, ever give in to the Coco Pops monster. I realise that my intransigence on this may well drive my children into cereal dens in later life, looking for a quick fix of Frosties while my back is turned. And I understand that my death will be accompanied by a massive out-pouring of milk onto some awful brown confection and I will be waked on chocolate Weetos. But that is the road I have chosen.)

On a less morbid note, no new year is now complete without all those dingbats sitting on deckchairs outside Budget Travel. There's no such thing as a free holiday, of course, and if the price of a package is the company of a dozen dull strangers for a Christmas spent on the pavement, then to my mind, that's way too high a price. That said, it's not so long since I believed that the saddest thing in the world would be to book a holiday in a different year from the one in which you intended taking it. Yet here we are, booked, suited, booted and ready to go in, oh, seven months or so. At least, by then The Small Girl should be able to draw her own bath so expertly we might hang it in a gallery.

BREAST, BEST

SMALL GIRL: 5 YEARS, 7 MONTHS
BOY: 3 YEARS, 6 MONTHS
BABY: 1 YEAR, 1 MONTH

In a single, brutal moment, my childbearing years are over. I'm thirty-six years old and the only things I've got to look forward to now are grandchildren and death.

Inevitably, I tried to prolong breastfeeding The Baby for as long as possible. The very mad part of my brain even fancied the idea of becoming one of those creepy mothers who silences the bus by suddenly lifting her jumper for the delectation and nutrition of an eight-year-old, but to my mind, there is a certain wardrobe that goes with that kind of militant maternity and I just didn't feel it would flatter me. I'm also quite partial to getting plastered from time to time and there isn't a breastfeeding manual in the world that gives that kind of carry-on a thumbs up (believe me, I've searched).

So once she turned a year (as she did just before Christmas), we were feeding on borrowed time. The older two weaned themselves around the year mark, more or less losing interest in the poor view afforded by breastfeeding. In addition, The Boy had started making the most of what would turn out to be his brief time in possession of two front teeth, so from a pain threshold perspective, I was glad to call that one a day.

But The Baby, the last by a long shot, showed no signs of quitting. And the mother, well, I was kind of loving it as well, those special, intimate, bonding moments that no formula can fake. The only cloud on our sunny delight was a contraceptive-shaped one. Not to put too fine a point on it, as long as the feeding continued there was always a chance that The Baby might be supplanted at the breast. And while that very mad bit was quite happy to continue filling the earth and conquering it, my obstetric record and its white-coated guardians have already ruled against another child. Not biologically impossible, but certainly irresponsible. Apparently the three we already have need me more than they let on.

So now that you know far more than you ever wanted to about my innards, we move on to last Saturday morning and the Final Feed. So often lately, these morning feeds have turned into snatched snacks to a soundtrack of 'Scooby Doo' and squabbling, but last weekend – through some miracle of timing – found the two home-wreckers lying in and the Nurturer and the Nurtured alone together for the last time. And so we passed a silent half-hour, utterly indulging each other, until, finally, she fell asleep for the final time on my breast and gently gave it up. I looked at her milky, sleeping face and, predictably, burst into tears.

Equally predictably, it took me all of about twelve hours and three cans of beer to inform The Husband that I wanted another baby. To his credit, his eyes didn't even flicker from the television as he assured me that that class of a ride was out of the question. He was quite right of course, but in the warm light of evening and alcohol, the end of six years of pregnancy, childbirth and breastfeeding was all too abrupt and – Heineken aside – there didn't immediately seem to be an awful lot there to take its place.

The Small Girl didn't help matters much in the days that followed. Questions like 'Was the President in your class at school when you were a little girl?' and observations about which sofa I should sit on to watch her being a pop star on television when I'm a 'very old lady' just conspired to make me feel that all the best bits were over.

Luckily, I'm way too shallow to be worried by these philosophical thoughts for long. By the middle of the week, the future once again seemed tantalising. The Baby has learnt to say 'Grandad' and has taken to spending long periods of the day sitting with her head in a bucket for no discernible reason. The Boy has made a new friend at playgroup and he's coming round on Friday with his green light sabre 'for a big fight'. And The Small Girl's pop star ambitions seem to have taken a large leap forward with the addition of the word 'wicked' to her vocabulary. Life goes on, even when every hormone in our bodies is screaming out to hold it back. I remember on my late grandmother's ninetieth birthday, buying her a greeting card with a large golden '90' on the front and an assurance inside that the best was yet to come. Of course, that was rubbish, but in a way, I know what Hallmark meant. When life gives you breasts, you make breast-milk. When they turn into lemons again, you've little choice but to make lemonade.

CROKE PARK

SMALL GIRL: 5 YEARS, 8 MONTHS
BOY: 3 YEARS, 7 MONTHS
BABY: 1 YEAR, 2 MONTHS

On the Sunday Supplement on Today FM, economist Moore McDowell does a quick sum and announces that half the country's population was born after the first moon landing. The Husband and I are decidedly in the wrong half, and we are about to age considerably more. Like a visit to the dentist, we've been putting it off for ages and making promises we'd only the vaguest intentions of keeping, but now the hour of reckoning has arrived: we are taking the two older kids to Croke Park for the first time.

Of course, this is not without baggage, both literal and figurative. My own first pilgrimage to Croker, taken when I was about The Boy's age, had a profound effect on me and set in motion a long love affair with Gaelic games, their headquarters and all that razzamatazz. The Dubs came later – back then, with a Corkman standing between myself and my brother, holding both our hands very firmly, we were destined for a rebel yell, if only for a short time. I can't remember who Cork played that day. I only know that when we walked up the steps of the Hogan Stand and saw the park for the first time, I recognised that life had suddenly got a whole lot better. My big brother, on the other hand, recognised that this was an opportunity for ice-cream almost unparalleled in his short life and hasn't been back since. These things affect different people in different ways.

I desperately wanted my kids to have an epiphany on a par with my own, but as we headed for Jones's Road, the omens were not good. A lively debate on whether the precipitation whipping around the car was hail, sleet or snow gave way, in short order, to the usual lament about the traffic and then an increasingly agitated search for a parking place. In the end, we found a likely spot just a short half-an-hour's walk from the ground, secured coats, hats, scarves and gloves and headed off. It's funny how different things look in the winter. It occurred to me, as we negotiated the north-side, that this is a part of the world that I can find my way around blindfold (and, on occasion, blind drunk) in summer sunshine, but stripped of foliage and warm glow, I had no idea where we were. Whisper it: I had to ask *directions* to Croke Park. Oh, the shame of it.

So we were very late, very cold and, in the case of the four littlest legs, very tired by the time we finally climbed the steps of the Cusack Stand (as an independent ticket-buyer I switched from the Hogan to the Cusack because the sun always shines on the Clon-liffe Road stand. I'd even brought my sunglasses. Oh, how we laughed). The Husband would have crashed straight in, but his-tory held me back, and so before we climbed those last steps, I dropped to my hunkers and told the small people that they would remember this moment for the rest of their lives. Then we walked into the light and a five-year-old and a three-year-old face con-firmed what I'd just promised. Magic.

Five minutes later – and in spite of all the GAA's spin – we were enmeshed in the grim reality of the league, watching bad football in worse weather. I had brought a huge bag of goodies, of course, and they were quickly called into service by two mittened kittens who insisted that their parents throw jelly tots and Barney crisps into their open mouths as the hail/sleet/snow poured down on their sorry heads. Midway through the second half, The Boy's violent teeth chattering gave way to quiet sobbing and I genuinely feared he would die of hypothermia. I took him out and into the ladies toilets, where I vigorously rubbed him all over till the sobs quietened and the mouth opened for Barney crisps once more. We left five minutes before the end and, like most of the Dubs (including the team), we were glad to go.

I won't even begin to describe the journey back to the car, or the hilarious and quickly abandoned detour to Gaffney's (more sobs from The Boy, massive strop from The Small Girl), or the certain relief which greeted the news that there'll be no more Croke Park jollies until April. It had been a fraught and frustrating day, but for that single moment, when two little Dubs saw the glory of their Croke Park for the first time, it has been worth it. On the way home, it occurred to me that my own first visit to Croker had happened around the same time as Neil Armstrong took his first small step. I don't remember the moon landing, but I'll never forget my own – and now my children's – giant leap. Maybe not the wrong half after all.

CROSSWORDS

SMALL GIRL: 5 YEARS, 8 MONTHS
BOY: 3 YEARS, 7 MONTHS
BABY: 1 YEAR, 2 MONTHS

I have often thought that the rather dreary feature in *Reader's Digest*, 'The Things Kids Say', could be significantly improved if they changed its name to 'The Things Kids Call Each Other' and altered its cloth accordingly. For its unique mix of energy, creativity and sheer stupidity, it is hard to beat juvenile cussing, and if I had my way, there'd be a whole magazine devoted to it, possibly with a free poo attached to the cover.

It's all going off at the moment in the Rainbow Playgroup, where I personally witnessed one of the boys calling an adult supervisor a 'shithead' just last week. This same three-year-old trooper has taken to calling my own boy a 'dope', to which he has responded by branding the offender a 'poo chute', which is an arsehole by any other name. I must admit that I was quite impressed by this one and even a little proud – although I'm pretty sure that it's a secondhand insult, and one quite possibly picked up from the Rainbow Warrior himself.

There was a similar contretemps a year ago, when The Small Girl tried to break up a schoolyard fight between two bigger boys and was rewarded for her trouble by being informed that she had a 'tiny head'. Aside from that, it's been pretty much 'peanut head' all the way in our house for a long time now, a choice insult and the insult of choice for the Nick Jr generation.

One of the few consolations of children getting older is that their swearing becomes absurdly ambitious, with suitably hilarious consequences. While small people are traditionally reluctant to expand their vocabularies in any practical way, they crave more and bigger bad words and are anxious to use them before they fully grasp their power. Just as adults like to use the words 'eclectic' and 'eponymous' without having any real clue what they mean, so I can remember, at the age of twelve, the word 'prostitute' arriving in the Annagaire Gaeltacht (*as Béarla*, mind) and several dozen youngsters spending three weeks exchanging sniggering jokes that none of us got. It was several years later – in my grandmother's kitchen, oddly enough – that it finally dawned on me what a prostitute was (it became clear in a joke my mother told my granny, cheeky) and in a flash, I suddenly understood about two dozen other jokes. I seem to recall that as a day of big laughs.

We might like to think of this precocious profanity as being peculiarly Irish, but I'd wager it's a universal phenomenon. The Husband, who is not from these parts, recalls a religion book of his youth (and this would be the Protestant religion, mind) which featured a drawing of Moses parting the Red Sea with his mighty staff. In his copy, the previous owner had drawn an arrow pointing to the top of the staff and had written the word 'brothel' beside it. In my own biology book, next to a large photo of a cross-section of a human testicle, marked 'one-seventh actual size', some more clued-in student had simply written 'Jesus Christ!' I remember another piece of choice graffiti from those days appearing on the last page of my copy of *Peig*, after a final chapter top-heavy with misery, poverty, death and depression. As Peig signed off by more or less saying that her appalling existence had in some way been a positive experience, the previous reader had added, in a fine hand, the words 'Jesus wept' to the final line.

By then, of course, we were learning irony and the halcyon days of immature swearing were already over. Far better, then, that we remember the fact that for two years in primary school, the word 'gee' was scrawled across the back of one of the toilet doors next to our classroom and that for those two years, at least five girls in my class were unable to use that toilet because they got too upset.

Or to recall the relay race on primary school sports day, when one of my classmates made the mistake of dropping the baton and was called a 'c***' by the competitive athlete who'd just passed it to her. Thus branded, the girl in question burst into tears, was unable to continue and our whole class was disqualified. We were later called upon to explain exactly what had happened, and partly because none of us had any idea what the c-word meant, we were at something of a loss.

Until a child learns the fact of life, they think defecation is the funniest thing in the whole world, with urination running it a close second. A whole new spectrum of profanity and humour opens up to them when they learn about those other bodily functions and emissions and nothing is ever quite as cute again. As far as my own kids are concerned, may the scatological years run and run. Which, come to think it if, is another word that adults tend to misuse. With even more hilarious consequences, I think you'll agree.

IF YOU'RE IRISH ...

SMALL GIRL: 5 YEARS, 9 MONTHS
BOY: 3 YEARS, 8 MONTHS
TODDLER: 1 YEAR, 3 MONTHS

The St Patrick's Day Parade killed my great-grandfather and I have had an ambivalent attitude towards it ever since. It never came to court, of course – and if it had, it's likely that the defence would have argued that it was less the parade itself than my great-grandfather's attending it without his overcoat that led to the pneumonia that ensured he never marked his fiftieth birthday. But legal argument cuts no dice with a four-year-old, so when I was heading out for my very first parade – and my grandmother cautioned me to wrap up well because her father had died as a direct result of being negligent in the overcoat department on just such a day as this – well, let's just say that all the baton twirling in the cosmos couldn't have salvaged that parade or any of the excruciating ones that followed it.

Aside from its decimation of my family, I had a second issue with the St Patrick's Day Parade. As a person of unimpressive stature – both then and now – I grew tired of staring at the back of strangers' (over)coats for two hours at a time, knowing that other people were having a grand old time just feet away from me. And frankly, I was never either patriotic or punctual enough to arrive at ten and spend two hours pressed against a barrier on the off-chance that some arsehole dressed as Ronald McDonald might deign to shake my hand.

But when the sun blasts down and you've been gifted grand-stand tickets, then it would be churlish not to give the parade another chance. In any event, we were on something of a roll in the family outing stakes, having had a successful collective splash in the National Aquatic Centre on its sneak preview day (at the start of which, I'm proud to say, The Baby became the first person in the country to piss in the national pool) and then an equally rewarding excursion to view the Skyfest fireworks last weekend. Admittedly, we'd a privileged position for that festivity as well, moonlighting in the rather grand city centre office of a member of my family, with a fire escape for the braver (The Family Member and The Small Girl) and a sturdier window for the wusses and the reckless (me, The Boy and, in the clutches of The Husband, The Baby, now officially re-classified as The Toddler.)

I'd never seen the Skyfest before, and I was pleased to note that in common with every fireworks display the world over, it was highly spectacular and about five minutes too long. Come to think of it, the only fireworks displays that are too short are the ones you have yourself in your back garden when you're drunk. Perhaps next year, the organisers of Skyfest might consider hiring some backyard genius to run the show and distribute free cans of Bulmers to the crowd in advance.

If the fireworks were five minutes too long, then it was reassur-ing to find that the parade, all these years later, is still half an hour over time. It also still has that irritating bit at the start, when loads of smug strangers drive by in mildly unconventional cars. This year, the cars were followed by what we were assured were the amazing skills of the Samba soccer school – I must admit that although our seats afforded us an infinitely better view than I'm used to, we still couldn't see anything that was happening in the six feet immediately above street level, so we had to take the commentator's word for it.

Later, we were happy to take the commentator's word again when he announced that 'taking up the rear are the Dublin Gay and Lesbian Collective'. To be honest, the entire trip was worth it for that heart-warming moment alone. In between times, there were some genuinely impressive displays (none of which seemed to be sponsored by Abel Alarms), a litany of bands, hardly any of which played as they passed us by, and loads of young girls in their knickers, which is always popular on our national day. Oh look, there's way too much bad blood between me and the St Patrick's Day Parade for me to ever enjoy it unreservedly, but The Small Girl – a generation further away from the doomed ancestor – was apoplectic with delight and declared the parade a success unparalleled. And The Boy, who can swing either way where entertainment is concerned, well, he had a fine time too, even if he spent the last half hour facing the wrong way and flapping his seat up and down.

Even The Husband, at his very first St Patrick's Day Parade, was pleasantly surprised (though he did fidget for that crucial last half hour). Then we left our grandstand behind and headed off into the blazing sunshine, buttoning up our overcoats as we went. Where the St Patrick's Day Parade is concerned, you can't be too careful.

GIRLS' TALK

SMALL GIRL: 5 YEARS, 11 MONTHS
BOY: 3 YEARS, 10 MONTHS
TODDLER: 1 YEAR, 5 MONTHS

If Joe Jackson (the singer, not the bearded journalist) really wants to hear Girls' Talk, then he could do worse than while an afternoon away in our back garden. My own favourite pursuit, of late, has been to find excuses to spend time outside – our patio has never been more scrupulously swept – in order to eavesdrop on The Small Girl discussing the issues of the day with her female friends.

The agenda of these meetings – all of which are held in the close environs of our swing, usually while one or other of the protagonists dangles upside down from the bar along the side – is as follows: their favourite colour; their place in the family and the amount of attention afforded to such a position; the most appropriate age at which to get their ears pierced.

The first of these topics engages The Small Girl the most. I must admit, I don't remember being as absorbed in the whole subject of colours and who favours what when I was five-going-on-six – in fact, I'm not even sure I *had* a favourite colour (oh, heresy!) – but other people's preferred colours rock The Small Girl's world and we've all had to row in accordingly. So we know that her favourite colour is pink (naturally), as is Anna's; Sarah's is orange and Rachel's is blue. Mine is green and Daddy's is red, and – get this! – Siobhán's daddy also favours red and her mammy loves green.

The Small Girl cares less about her position in the family, though Anna, the youngest, is very worried about hers. She feels she doesn't get enough attention and, as evidence to support her complaint, offers the fact that on her sister's Confirmation Day she got less attention than her sister. Rachel is also the youngest in her family, though to be honest, she feels she probably gets a bit too much attention.

Rachel's also just got her ears pierced – an event that has moved the whole earrings issue higher up the agenda. Anna's not rushing into anything, but The Small Girl would have hers done right now – hanging upside down from the swing if necessary – if only her heartless harridan of a mother would let her. I've told the applicant that she can get them done for her Confirmation, but as she's pointed out, she'll be really old by then and everyone else in the world will have them done before her. (If I may briefly return from the garden to my soapbox, this kind of pressure is most unfair on parents. Readers will be aware of my fascistic position on Coco Pops. Now, I'm ashamed to admit that persistent pressure from The Boy – he's taken to standing in front of the cereal display in the supermarket, sighing audibly – has resulted in a partial climb down on my part, and we will be purchasing Coco Pops during the summer holidays with the agreement that they are not to be consumed at breakfast time. If I go the same way with the pierced ears thing, The Small Girl's likely to have one done in time for her Communion.)

Back in the more forgiving outdoors, I confess that I adore these little women and their weighty conversation. I can't really remember what we talked about BB (Before Boys), but I'd like to think that the conversations were as innocent and as earnest as the ones I'm now privileged to overhear in my own back garden. It will only be a couple of short years before their thoughts turn to young men, and when they do, the hard-line mother will no longer be allowed to listen in. The meetings will readjourn on the green at the end of the road and (pierced) ears will burn at the merest mention of the name of the Dish of the Day.

In the meantime, aware that childhood and innocence are brutally short, I reserve my right to be a nosey parker. As my children get older, I'm increasingly horrified at the acceleration of their development, and so I want to spend as much time as possible lurking round the swing with the chattering classes.

But we can't hold back progress. In the middle of a tuna sandwich over the weekend, The Small Girl announced that her tooth felt funny. Examination showed that the tiny tooth – the first to break through her gums just over five years ago – is loose. As I watched it wobble, I suddenly (and most unexpectedly) burst into tears. My first-born, my tiniest baby, and here she is about to dispense with her first perfect baby tooth. I stood in front of her, sobbing, while she regarded me as though I were mad. 'It's only a tooth,' she pointed out. She's quite right. At this rate, when she starts menstruating, I'll spontaneously combust. In a glorious display, one hopes, of all her favourite colours.

FAMILY ADVERTISING

SMALL GIRL: 5 YEARS, 11 MONTHS
BOY: 3 YEARS, 10 MONTHS
TODDLER: 1 YEAR, 5 MONTHS

Fond as I am of Superquinn, the worst ad on the radio at the moment has to be the one for the supermarket chain's new Waitrose meals range. Lest you haven't had the privilege, it goes something like this: chirpy mother enquires of family – husband and more children than I can count – what they'd like for their dinner; happy family respond by each demanding a different dish, everything from pizza to Thai chicken; chirpy mum assures them that this long and varied menu will present her with no difficulty, given (presumably) that her fridge is positively groaning with Waitrose meals; they all live happily ever after.

I hate this ad on a number of levels. I hate the mother for being daft enough to give her family a choice at meal times. I hate the family for being cheeky enough to respond with such an eclectic selection. I hate the children for being sophisticated enough to demand anything besides chicken nuggets. Above all, I hate the fact that the mother's reaction to these unreasonable demands is to sunnily accommodate them, when surely the correct response would be to tell them all to shag off and take herself off to a snug of her choice.

Advertising creates unrealistic standards for mothers. Dads are generally portrayed as a collection of Tims-Nice-But-Dim, hapless sorts who can't sort out a washing load but like going to McDonald's. But mothers are presented as good-humoured human dynamos, more washing cycle than menstrual cycle, all heart and Sunny Delight. The dynamo bit I don't have a problem with, but I must take serious issue with the perpetual bonhomie of these fictional females. Real mothers understand that there's a hell of a lot of shitty jobs associated with running a household, and accordingly perform them with a measure of bad grace.

Or at least, this one does. You know that woman whose young son kicks a muddy football at her washing line and leaves a perfect imprint of the ball on her clean white sheets? In washing powder ad-land, the mother just sighs in a Boys-Will-Be-Boys way and does the washing again. In my world, that misdemeanour would result in a scene akin to the crucifixion in the garden but with a great deal more bad language.

Indeed, The Boy in my world already behaves like most small boys in ads do, even if I refuse to play my part. Just the other day, for example, he and his TV-ad cute girlfriend went rummaging in the press for something edible and, instead, knocked an almost full bottle of balsamic vinegar with a dodgy lid over onto its side. As the dark liquid pooled out into the press, creating miniature islands out of bags of rice and pasta and packets of cream crackers, they must have considered their options and decided that since I was in the other room, their crime could go undetected. They closed the press and it was only when the vinegar started seeping out under the door and spreading across the floor that they decided to call in the cavalry. I was alerted to the fact that there was a ''mergency' in the kitchen, and arrived on the scene in time to turn the air over the dark brown floor blue. The Boy is well-used to this kind of carry-on, of course, but his girlfriend seemed suitably horrified and asked – not unreasonably – to be allowed go home.

The point is that, had this ''mergency' happened in an ad, I would have cast my eyes up to heaven with a smile, congratulated the pair of tousle-haired conspirators (The Boy isn't tousle-haired at all, but if he were in an ad, he would be) and rewarded the whole family with a round of Sunny D and eight different types of ready meals. In the unreal world, that gobshite who pushes Flash products would probably have even come in to clean up the mess.

The only ad whose portrayal of family appeals to me is the one for pasta sauce, in which an Italian family prepare a huge pot of spaghetti and then sit down to enjoy it together with a glass of wine. Chiefly, I like it because it's not just the mother stoically preparing the meal. Of course, it's this that also makes it wholly unbelievable, even before the cute little boy polishes off his whole plate without getting a drop of tomato sauce on his white shirt.

Because we are not Italian and because we are not in an ad, in this house, when we eat spaghetti Bolognese The Boy needs to be hosed down afterwards. Luckily – also because we are not Italian – we've usually resorted to binge drinking by the end of the meal, and then we don't feel so bad.

BIG BIG MOVIE

SMALL GIRL: 5 YEARS, 11 MONTH
BOY: 3 YEARS, 10 MONTHS
TODDLER: 1 YEAR, 5 MONTHS

There's a kind of hush that descends on our home every Saturday evening round about teatime. Parents of young children right across the country enjoy a similar respite from the hurdy-gurdy of family life at the same time, same channel. The time is 6.30pm, the channel RTÉ 1 and the cause of this national ceasefire is billed as 'The Big Big Movie'.

It's a piece of inspired scheduling. A children's film to bond the family just at the time when the household and the whole weekend tends to fall apart. In our home, it is recognised as a sort of traditional weekly coming together, children down one end of the family room congregating round a bowl of popcorn, parents up the other with a bottle in one hand and back-up in the fridge. And in the green corner, something with Robin Williams in it or a robot or some cute but unnaturally talented animal. And we all live happily ever after.

Except that sometimes I wonder about the person in RTÉ who chooses the Big Big Movie. Last weekend, it was *Look Who's Talking*, a charming enough comedy that relaunched the career of

John Travolta and in the process found a way for Bruce Willis to appear in major feature films without being annoying. So far, so cheesy popcorn.

And so to the plot. Kirstie Alley plays a single woman who gets pregnant by a married man. Married man clearly has no plans to leave his wife and children so taxi driver Travolta steps into the breech, helping Alley through the labour and birth and becoming a father figure for the baby. Inevitably, they fall in love and have sex while the baby sleeps.

Now, excuse me if I come across like the Alice Glenn of the rock 'n' roll generation, but how on earth can that be construed as a children's film? I'm not a prude, but (in fact, if you can preface every line from here till the end with those words, you'll save me the ink) in the first ten minutes of the film, there was a scene in which millions of talking and very determined sperm swam towards an egg. Now, while images like this cause the adults down the end of the room nothing worse than shuddering flash-backs, it's not exactly ideal viewing material for the popcorn munchers closer to the screen. Don't get me wrong – it's not that I have any problem with films that acknowledge the process of pro-creation; I just kind of wish I hadn't forced three children under the age of six to watch them.

Of course, while The Toddler couldn't have cared less if the entire cast had it off in front of her as long as the popcorn supply wasn't affected, we have now entered the tricky area of What-The-Hell-Do-You-Tell-The-Kids with the other two. In fact, we had a double dose of it this week. My best friend's adorable, furniture-munching puppy has suddenly developed into some sort of canine sex siren and before she could get used to that kind of thing, she was dispatched to the vet's to be neutered. 'Millie's having an operation,' their boy told ours on the way to playgroup.

'They're going to cut her open and give her stitches and you can't touch her.'

Well, that might have been good enough for their boy but it most assuredly wasn't sufficient for ours. But *why* is Millie being cut open, he demanded. Eh … it's just a small operation, I countered. But what's wrong with her? Eh … nothing. 'She's getting stitches and you can't touch her,' their boy reiterated impatiently and for a while, that was that. But The Boy told The Small Girl and she too was unhappy with the quality of information supplied. And then suddenly John Travolta and Kirstie Alley were making the beast with the two backs right in front of them. Sweet Jesus, what kind of a world do we live in?

We're actually pretty modern (or embarrassing, depending on your perspective) on the whole childbirth thing: partly because they have a baby sister, the two older ones know how babies develop, where it all happens and even the orifice that the result emerges from. But we have been appropriately vague on the subject of how it gets in there in the first place. When we're asked (as we inevitably were in the first ad break of The Big, Big Movie, even as Captain Bird's Eye was inviting the kids to solve his riddle) I mutter stuff about Holy God and The Husband goes for a shower. But it is a short-term solution only, and soon – however much we might hope to put it off – we're going to have to get our stories straight about life, the universe and canine hysterectomies. Alternatively, of course, we can just sit them down in front of children's television and let RTÉ do the honours for us.

WAITING LISTS

SMALL GIRL: 6 YEARS, 2 MONTHS
BOY: 4 YEARS, 1 MONTH
TODDLER: 1 YEAR, 8 MONTHS

I have just put The Small Girl's name down for secondary school. She is, after all, six. What is even more alarming/depressing is that I've also alerted the school to the existence of The Toddler, lest they be planning for the future and might somehow have left her out.

There is something entirely insane about filling in any form and writing the date 2014 on it. It's up there with writing your address and failing to stop at the country – just as smart-aleck kids place themselves in The World, The Galaxy, The Solar System, The Universe, so applying for a place in a school for 2014 seems to be taking the piss.

I mean, will there be schools at all in 2014? Or will we all be living in biospheres on faraway planets, with only the last three lines of our childhood addresses remaining the same? Anything could happen between now and then: we might all be wiped out by a runaway Luas; the school in question might switch from All-Girl to All-Gay; or we might join a cult that believes in educating children in trees.

On the other hand, the nineteen years since I left school have passed so fast that I can only assume that the next eleven years will be done and dusted in the space of a couple of months. I should probably get her uniform just in case.

When we lived in London, the posh women I knocked around with were obsessed with the merits of different schools. As soon as our collective stitches healed, while our first-born were still puking on our shoulders, half of them already had their babies' names down at the top secondary schools in the country. One mother had specifically chosen a school because it had a reputation for being particularly strong on languages, and all the indications were that her son was leaning towards that area. That the child in question hadn't at that stage spoken a single word in any language and that as far as I could tell, the only thing he leant towards was the sideboard, hadn't deterred his parents from making a career choice on his behalf. It wasn't so much an educated guess as an education guess.

So then we came home to a country where nobody gave two hoots about which school their children went to as long as they stayed out of the house for the best part of the day, and suddenly I'm bludgeoned again by parents putting tiny people's names down for very big schools left, right and centre.

It's a class thing, of course. It is only posh people whose To Do list in life reads, 'Conceive, put name down for Gonzaga, give birth'. The kind of people I grew up with – and am largely still surrounded by – are content for nature and the state school system to take their course. As a result, they're spared years of worrying whether or not they should have put their offspring's name down for a certain school while they themselves were still a pupil there. Of course, most impressive schools now charge a registration fee in the region of €500 just to add Junior's name to the list. Sometimes I wonder how the people who have money in this country manage to keep hold of it at all at all.

So I should point out that the only reason I've put the girls' names down is because we want them to go to a single-sex secondary school and the one they'd automatically filter into is a co-ed establishment. The school we've chosen is all-girl, close by and free, which were pretty much the only criteria we used. There was also the indisputable fact that when I was growing up, the girls from this particular school seemed to be much better-looking than we were and always bagged the best-looking boys. Not a completely sound premise on which to select a school for your own children, I'll grant you, but a far better idea than putting an aspirational child's name down for every school that ever made it to a Leinster Schools' Cup final and paying €500 a throw for the pleasure.

Which brings me to The Boy. No, is the answer. By the time we returned to Ireland he was already eighteen months old and so, I gather, had missed the cut-off point for all the impressive schools. Besides, while we want the girls simply to be educated amongst women, I want The Boy to attend a school that excels at Gaelic games, doesn't have mucky clergymen on the staff, will encourage his creativity and doesn't accept the kind of boys who batter other boys at bus stops. Since such an establishment doesn't exist, I may have to set it up myself. Anyone wishing to have their boys taught in trees, come join me.

LOVE BITES

SMALL GIRL: 6 YEARS, 4 MONTHS
BOY: 4 YEARS, 3 MONTHS
TODDLER: 1 YEAR, 10 MONTHS

I have begun to disgust my daughter. In a way, I can't say I blame her. I am currently sporting a love-bite, a present from The Husband for my thirty-seventh birthday. I also got an anorak, though I'm bringing that back and changing it for something that doesn't make me look like a lesbian on a bin tax protest. Would that I could do the same with the love-bite.

It's sod's law that I never had love-bites when they mattered, when they might have impressed my peers. Almost everyone else in my school seemed to have scuffles with vampirical adolescent boys on a weekly basis, and come Monday they'd all show up wearing scarves to cover up their scarred necks which were then proudly revealed in the toilets. The less fortunate amongst us – the unloved – would stare in horror and envy at these mottled necks, all the while lamenting our own deep veins/ lack of boyfriends.

I always assumed it was the former that prevented me from getting similarly bitten, but with hindsight I can now conclude that it was more to do with a lack of enthusiasm on the part of my young suitors. Because when I was in my mid-twenties – far too old to show them off in the toilets – I met a man with an appetite for destruction and suddenly I was covered in hickies. They, like him, eventually went away and I thought I'd done with love-bites – two decades of action compressed into one night – until this week. I suppose I should be ashamed of myself, but I've put in too many love-bite free miles not to rejoice in the tiny red mark on my neck. You might even have seen it on television this week. *That's* how proud I am.

As it happens though, it's not the love-bite that is causing The Small Girl so much offence (partly because she hasn't noticed it, the heartless cur). The other day I left a magazine on the kitchen table, opened at a fashion spread that included some pretty pink lingerie, and as soon as The Small Girl saw it, she announced it was ''sgusting'. What's disgusting? I ventured. 'Bras and knickers.' Why are bras and knickers disgusting? 'Because you wear them.'

Meanwhile, she has started to raise her eyes to heaven when The Husband and I kiss or canoodle in front of her, and if he says something that suggests he finds me in any way desirable, she laughs her head off. If it weren't for the consoling fact that The Boy thinks I'm absolutely gorgeous, I might be insecure about it.

But I understand that The Small Girl, at the grand old age of six, has taken her first steps down a road that will end with her sitting round with her friends discussing whether or not their parents still 'do it' and being genuinely appalled at the idea they've ever done it at all. I don't know why it is part of the human condition to feel so queasy at the suggestion that parents are sexual beings, but even the most enlightened of us has a problem with the visuals that suggests. Why should this be? Is it to prevent us having sex with our parents (and if so, how come it's failed so spectacularly in parts of rural Ireland)?

I remember my own mother having a pregnancy scare when I was a teenager and my being absolutely mortified by the experience. It wasn't the prospect of another, much younger mouth at the trough that bothered me so much as the implication that my parents had had sex at any time in the previous decade. Even now, the memory sends a shudder down my spine and I can only hope that by this stage they really have given it up for good (and if you're reading this, mother, please don't ever, ever even hint that this may not be the case).

Of course, it may all have to do with respect. Last week's *Irish Times* Youth Poll found that people between the ages of fifteen and twenty-four respect their parents more than anyone else – which presumably is news to the parents in question, and something of a shock to the rapper, 50 Cent. Perhaps it's impossible to respect people that we suspect of having a robust sex life (which might explain why the Taoiseach finished so low in the poll), and so we collectively reject our parents' sexuality in order that we can look them in the eye and name-check them in an *Irish Times* poll.

Or maybe it's a family affair, and what goes around comes around. That ad for Smirnoff, in which the young man informs his prospective father-in-law that his intentions are 'as honourable as yours were' has struck a universal chord, tapping into the horror we have of our children becoming sexually active. Back in our disgusting home, we're some years away from having to deal with our children's sexuality in any real or unpleasant way, but already The Husband has made it clear that he'll be shooting his daughters' suitors on sight. I must admit that I have no real difficulties with the idea of any of my children frolicking in fields with unsavoury sorts, but I say that from the safe distance of a decade or so and I absolutely reserve the right to change my mind and load the gun for The Husband come the glorious day. Besides, one of them might come home with a serious love-bite and open up those teenage wounds again. And all the name checks in all the *Irish Times* polls in the world won't be able to compensate for that.

FOOTBALL DREAMS

SMALL GIRL: 6 YEARS, 4 MONTHS
BOY: 4 YEARS, 3 MONTHS
TODDLER: 1 YEAR, 10 MONTHS

My life to date has been pretty much geared towards the day my son will lift the Sam Maguire for Dublin, but four weeks into The Boy's formal training with the GAA, I am beginning to wonder if I should find myself some new ambitions.

It is not that he is a bad footballer; it is just that he isn't a footballer at all. He is a kisser and a cuddler, and has become an expert in tucking the legs of his football shorts into his underpants so that he appears to be wearing some sort of vile pantaloons. He is also very good at falling over, facing the wrong way and abandoning matches at crucial points in order to climb a tree or urinate on its trunk. Last weekend, he even managed to go to the toilet during his stint in goal. Sad to report, his absence didn't make one shred of difference to the proceedings.

My own role in all of this is to shout at him a lot while silently wishing he didn't love me quite so much. The other boys spend the time between their drills and their solo runs wrestling each other pointlessly; The Boy celebrates each successful drill by running over to me for a kiss and a hug. If he were playing soccer, his desire for constant congratulatory lip contact might be more acceptable, but this is the GAA, for God's sake. They do things different here

For one thing, there is a peculiar hierarchy at play. While The Boys run around, fall over and occasionally kick the ball (I understand that passing it is something we can't realistically expect until they reach puberty), the mothers stand to one side watching the skies and wondering about washing. The fathers, meanwhile, are drafted in to help train the boys. Even The Husband, a foreigner and a Liverpool supporter, is given training duties when he brings The Boy. So even as the Ladies Gaelic Football Association celebrates its most successful season ever, the old guard still leaves the ball-handling to the men.

In my own case, this is probably just as well. The first time I took The Boy to his training session, he ran out on the astroturf (how posh is that?), picked up a ball and threw it to me. I caught it and then glanced down at the words 'Gaelic football' printed across it. And I suddenly realised, that after thirty-seven years of following the game, occasionally to ridiculous lengths, this was the first time I'd ever touched a Gaelic football.

I belong to a generation – to the last generation – of Irish women whose role in the GAA was perceived as being a sandwich-making one. When I was growing up, girls simply didn't play the game. In any case, the established fact that I was astonishingly bad at every other sport I attempted didn't augur well for any glorious career in Gaelic football, so I happily became the Roger Vadim of the national game: I just liked to watch.

But my own daughters will play it, simply because the school is big on it, and bigger again on hurling. I love the fact that they will have the same opportunities in the GAA as The Boy, and if The Small Girl isn't already training, it's only because she's far more interested in speech and drama and like her mother before her, she has already displayed a happy hopelessness in all sports attempted.

But The Boy likes the idea of football and he boasts the size and strength to suggest he might even be quite good at it. Unfortunately, nothing else whatsoever about him backs that up. Watching him on the training pitch, it's clear that though he has a dream, it has nothing whatsoever to do with the Sam Maguire. It is more concerned with the shape of the clouds, the possibility of rabbits and whether or not such a thing as Star Wars runners exist.

So while the other, smaller boys of St Jude's under-fives' race around after the ball, half-killing themselves and each other in its pursuit, The Boy faces the other way and occasionally waves. I, meanwhile, run along the sideline shouting instructions at him as though it were already the All Ireland Final and I some kind of tortured *bainisteoir*, and when the other tiny players score I cheer them loudly and wish they were mine. You should know that I am the only person who does this.

But I am not the only person who sees a direct line between the under-fives Saturday training session and All Ireland glory. All the men and women in all the clubs around the country who willingly give up their lie-ins and their days off in order to drill four-year-olds in Gaelic football without any money changing hands know, in the back of their minds, that everything they do today is about a glimmer of a far-off tomorrow. The GAA (rightly) takes plenty of flak from people suspicious of its motives, but at this, astroturf level, its motives are selfless and absolutely pure. Somewhere in the St Jude's under-fives there may well be a Jason Sherlock or a Ciarán Whelan.

Unfortunately – and you've no idea how much it pains me to admit this – it's not The Boy. Though God knows, we'll keep trying. Coming away from training last Saturday, we talked about how he'll play for the Dubs when he grows up. 'And on the day of the All Ireland final,' says I, 'Do you know who'll be the proudest person sitting in the Hogan Stand?' He beamed up at me, poised for yet another kiss. 'Me,' he said.

I am reviewing the situation.

NAPPIES

SMALL GIRL: 6 YEARS, 5 MONTHS
BOY: 4 YEARS, 4 MONTHS
TODDLER: 1 YEAR, 11 MONTHS

On the day The Small Girl was born, her tiny three-and-a-half pound body was quickly enveloped in an unfeasibly small nappy which she, with similar efficiency, immediately filled with the most astonishingly foul substance known to man. In the six-and-a-half years that have passed since then, there hasn't been a single day when I haven't changed a nappy. At the time of writing, I reckon I've used some 9,855 nappies on three bottoms. You know that ad for Pampers where the baby figures out where to put the balls while he sleeps? I paid for that. And the one before it, where the little darling crawls across the wooden floor at high speed? Yep, I reckon that one was mine as well.

But there is light at the end of the padded tunnel. If Pampers are planning next year's staff outing on the presumption that our family will continue to contribute so significantly to its coffers, then it had better go for a chicken-in-a-basket do on the wrong side of the M50. Shout it from the rooftops: we have taken the first baby steps towards toilet training The Toddler. We still have some way to go before we can look the bin-men in the eye again, but after six-and-a-half years and almost 10,000 nappies, we are finally on the home straight.

So why do I feel more like drowning sorrows than popping champagne corks? Changing a nappy is hardly one of life's high-lights – and on a bad day, it can be a sort of toxic hell on earth – so why am I not now clicking my heels in anticipation of emancipa-tion?

It's because I'm mad, of course. The cutting of the cord between our family and the Pampers Corporation (it was only a cottage industry when we first came across it) heralds far more than a busy time for the washing machine. A house without nappies is a home without a baby, and we've never known that round here. The Small Girl and The Boy were toilet trained without sentiment because in both cases another baby had come along to soak up the wayward hormones that such a significant life-change releases. In fact, we'd very little over-lapping on the nappy front, with both the older kids electing to put away foolish things within weeks of seeing someone so much less capable languishing in smaller nappies. But now, there is no usurper, no pitter-patter to embarrass The Toddler into knickers and to reassure her mother that life isn't speeding up into a gallop.

So there were lots of tears in the kitchen the other night when she was forced, not without protest, into a pair of tiny knickers. Mainly, those tears were hers, but they quickly dried up when she examined her new look, flexed her pudgy legs and strutted happily around for a while 'like Ciara'. More like her than she knew, as it happened, since the knickers in question were a cast-off pair from The Small Girl, who could probably still squeeze into them as well. Undoubtedly, they were a more snug fit on her firmer sister, who kept bending over to get a closer look, before she eventually wet them and then sat on her potty to celebrate. Like I said, first steps.

But all the time she was strutting, I was watching my baby's bum and quietly, sadly accepting that my kids are growing up. The following morning, I was issuing instructions to The Small Girl, who was going to a friend's house after school for a play and who wouldn't be home till tea-time, and she suddenly hugged me and said 'Poor Mam, soon we'll be all gone away.'

I can console myself with the knowledge that if it is too soon, there'll be a huge amount of little accidents. Of course, one of the reasons for my sudden affection for nappies might be because I know only too well that the disposal of nappies heralds an era of panic; of dashing to dirty toilets in shopping centres, of carrying spare underwear and squelchy shoes, of being unable to have a meal in a restaurant without a trip to the toilet every five minutes or so. At least this time, I won't have the double jeopardy of a baby in a sling round my neck just poised to be tipped into a strange toilet.

The other reason for the sudden sentimentality is that although we've got through a hell of a lot of them, they were never nappies in our home. They were and in memory will always be 'pangers'. The word was given to me by my mother, but was coined by my paternal grandmother – who died before I was born – and was a Kerry woman's interpretation of 'pannier', because first thing in the morning, a sodden nappy dropped down like a donkey's pannier. I love that word, the sound of it as well as the symbolism, and I loved the unexpected contribution that a grandmother I never met made to my modern family.

But while the phasing out of pangers might have stirred up some unexpected emotion, in the long-term, it's a development to be welcomed. There's no time to dwell on sentimentality because, as The Small Girl pointed out, soon they'll be all gone away. In the meantime, there are lots and lots of cuddles to be had, kisses to be stolen and, for a little while longer, beautiful bottoms to be admired. And in the short term, there's some underwear to be bought. If there's one thing I've learnt in life, it's that every girl should have her own knickers.

CHRISTMAS TOYS

SMALL GIRL: 6 YEARS, 7 MONTHS
BOY: 4 YEARS, 6 MONTHS
TODDLER: 2 YEARS, 1 MONTH

If I might be so bold, a suggested New Year's resolution for toy manufacturers: finish your bloody toys! I have just spent an entire Christmas season with my head bowed over a succession of half-made toys. I don't mind putting in batteries, but since when was it supposed to be up to the parents to actually make the toy? I realise you people in the Far East probably get paid about ten cent a day to assemble these things, but must you take it out on my family? Christ, have we not suffered enough?

So lo, it came to pass that I spent the first hour of Christmas morning assembling a Beyblade. A Beyblade, if you are lucky enough to be over the age of eight or childless, is a small spinning top that retails at €8.99 and is inordinately popular with young men. My young man was so good this year that Santa checked twice and brought him two of them. Only when he opened the boxes, they fell out on little plastic frames for mammies and daddies to make. So while the kids shrieked in excitement and The Husband cursed the logic that makes Mattel secure every single one of Barbie's belongings with plastic-coated metal wire (why? are they likely to flee?), I sat on our distressed mahogany chest in my dressing gown, my arse going increasingly numb, and tried to insert Gear Drive A into Metal Shaft B while clicking Pin Blades A and C into position. An hour later, I was finished, and I'd even managed to save a piece for later. This, though, was the centrifugal force generator or some such shite and so The Husband had to step in, disassemble the whole thing and put it together again with added gravity. It took another hour. It is tiny. The Boy played with it for ten minutes.

I didn't dare go near the second Beyblade and even The Husband opted to leave it for a day or two. In the end, though, he sat at the kitchen table and opened the little box. Three hours later, he was still at it. This is a man who can build a working radio from washing-up liquid bottles, who has constructed an entire recording studio from sticky-backed plastic. And a Beyblade nearly killed him. When he had finally finished it, he showed me the instructions. Half laughing, half crying, he indicated the final picture in the incredibly complex diagram. This is what your Beyblade should look like, it said. It looked like nothing on earth and in that, at least, the picture hadn't lied.

But the hell didn't end there. A simple game of Buckaroo was opened and we discovered we had to make the mule ourselves. Why? Why couldn't MB Games have gone the extra mile and made the mule? The Winnie-the-Pooh picnic table was just a bunch of bags and a load of pictures with arrows connecting them. The Power Rangers were (and still are) a mysterious collection of angry-looking bits that no instructions could becalm. Meanwhile, a friend down the road had to call into his next door neighbour's house at midnight on Christmas Eve with a bottle of wine in one hand and some hideous male contraption in the other and solicit help with a cry of 'You've an engineering degree, don't you?'

At least we only have one boy. Girls' toys are altogether simpler, for some reason. The Mini Baby Born had actually been born, the Barbie stuff was already assembled before it was firmly secured to its packaging. But all the mad stuff that boys like seems to arrive in inexplicable bits. I am bewildered enough by boys' toys without having to build them myself. I mean, what the hell is a Zord? I have looked it up in the dictionary and even it doesn't know. And yet Zords and Mega-Zords seem to rock young boys' worlds. And now, in spite of the fact that I haven't a clue what they are, I am expected to make them from scratch and pay for the privilege. Whose fabulous idea is that?

We are at a stage now where toys have become the polar opposite of paint: if Ronseal does exactly what it says on the tin, then our children's playthings no longer look anything like what it says on the box. We are about to invest in a new washing machine and I am presuming that when we open the box, it will already resemble, however fleetingly, a washing machine. But Beyblades that look like nothing and Buckaroo mules that are of interest only to Damien Hirst are now the staples of toy life. No wonder people complain about children today being lazy – how could it be any other way when the very people charged with keeping them amused can't be bothered going the extra mile and finishing what they started?

Our personal Christmas adventure in toyland was further complicated by the fact that both our older children asked for toys that don't actually exist. I'm all in favour of little ones using their imagination but when it extends to a Power Rangers bouncy castle, then it's no fun for anyone. The Toddler, meanwhile, is still gazing in beatific wonder at the vast number of small houses, complete with tiny residents, that have come her way and added to her already bustling village of plastic dwellings. It's a small town now; so much so that they're expecting a government department to descend on it any day, complete with a tiny minister. Now why does transport seem the most likely candidate?

THE ONE WHO DIDN'T MAKE IT
(Published January 2004)

*I discovered I was pregnant for the second time on my very first
Mother's Day. It was unplanned and unwanted, and when the
blue line appeared in the window on the pregnancy test, I burst
into tears. All on my own in the bathroom, while my husband
and our eight-month-old baby daughter plotted an inaugural
Mother's Day treat in the kitchen. She had been born two
months premature and our shared life so far had been tough.
She was still in newborn baby clothes, still on antibiotics and I
was still breastfeeding. I was exhausted. The last thing I needed
was another pregnancy and another baby.*

*I dried my tears and went into the kitchen. As soon as I heard
the words, 'Happy Mother's Day,' addressed to me for the very
first time, I was off again. In between sobs, I told him I was pregnant. He was as shocked and dismayed as I was. When we'd all
calmed down, he said he felt that we were being cheated out of
our time with an only child. I just wondered how I'd cope with
another baby and I lay awake all that night worrying about it,
just me and my unwanted baby.*

*When did he become wanted? Over the next few days and
weeks, while he grew inside me, he somehow found his way into
our hearts. Two children under eighteen months started to seem
less daunting – even, just possibly, an occasion of joy. We
guessed he might be a boy – no reason, just a hunch – and we
wondered how he'd get along with his tiny big sister. We told
friends and family who slagged us for being nymphomaniacs,
who rejoiced with us in anticipation of the chaos ahead. They
all told me to take it easy and some advised me to give up*

breastfeeding. I couldn't do the first and I didn't want to do the second.

At the hospital, they performed an early dating scan – the breastfeeding had knocked my menstrual cycle off its calendar and I'd no idea when I'd conceived. An early dating scan is conducted internally, and is a horrible and invasive procedure – but in the middle of it all, while my dignity was suspended, there he suddenly was on the screen. And there was his tiny heart, beating like a little piston in his barely formed chest. It was a strong and regular beat. And when I saw it, just as I had done when I'd first heard my daughter's heart, I closed my eyes and made a simple prayer: let it still be beating long after my own has stopped.

But it didn't. A week later, going to bed on a Saturday night, something felt wrong. I honestly can't explain what. I wasn't in pain, I had no discharge, but somehow, I knew. The last thing I said to my husband before we went to sleep was 'something's wrong with the baby'. The following morning, I saw that I had bled a little in the night and I knew my baby had died.

At the hospital, though, they weren't so sure. Lots of women bleed slightly in pregnancy, they told me; there really wasn't any reason to fear the worst. Hope surged in my miserable body as they wheeled me to the top floor for another scan. Same drill as before. Only this time, the faces of the technicians told me the result was different. They asked me if I wanted to see him and I said I did. There he was, a tiny thing, a perfect little body lying on his side. And no piston, no heartbeat. 'I'm so sorry,' the obstetrician said, 'your baby has died.' He had lived for just ten weeks, which isn't very long. But it was a lifetime.

The next few days are a bit of a blur. Lots of advice, loads of literature, lots of reassurance. Not my fault. Nothing to do with the breastfeeding. Nature's way of dealing with its mistakes.

Nobody said anything about my not wanting him in the first place, because by then, I think everyone understood that I wanted him more than anything else in the world. And I still do.

Three days after the scan, I returned to the hospital for a procedure called an Evacuation and Removal of Conception Product. Conception Product. That's what my baby had become. The staff were as sensitive as people who deal with a dozen of these a day can be, but there was a brutality about the whole business, the language, the lack of emotion. All my charts stated that I'd had an 'involuntary abortion', a description which seemed to me another kick in my aching abdomen. When I came around from the operation, a wonderful nurse took my hand and asked me how I was. 'Okay,' I muttered through the fading anaesthetic, 'not much pain.' 'No,' she repeated, changing the emphasis on her words: 'how are you?' More tears, more pain.

And more questions. Why me? Was it something I'd done? Something I hadn't done? And would it happen again?

And in between the questions, life went on. I minded my baby, kept my house, wrote my jokes. I didn't miss a column deadline. Those who hadn't known about the baby never knew about the miscarriage – in the six years since it happened, this is the first time I've ever mentioned it in public. Well, you don't, do you? And yet, experts estimate that as many as one in four pregnancies ends in miscarriage. It is as common as brown-eyed babies, and yet miscarriage remains a taboo subject, a harbinger of awkward silences. You can't be seen to grieve too much, because then you might undermine the pain of parents who've lost children who were born and breathed. It was only ten weeks, after all. Not even a belt notch. Other women don't talk about it, so you too hide it away. Hardly a life, hardly a death.

But the grief is real, the bereavement is real and the tears were real. And the guilt – God, the guilt. Was it because we didn't want him enough in the beginning? Was it because our good news seemed like such bad news at the time? Was it the breastfeeding? All you can do is grieve and research. The first helps the heart, the second assuages the guilt. It was nothing we did or didn't do; it could happen to anyone and it does happen to one in three women. We were just unlucky, the research said. But we weren't. We have our health, our lives and three perfect children. It was our tiny, nameless baby who was unlucky.

And life still goes on. Five months after my miscarriage, I was pregnant again. I didn't tell anyone until I was so obviously pregnant that people didn't need to be told. At the hospital, they gave out to me for not coming to them sooner, but I had my reasons. And now I have a big, strapping son who I wouldn't have if I hadn't lost a baby. You can tie yourself up in knots with logic like that, but sometimes it helps. We planted a rose bush in memory of our baby who had no name and no grave, and when we moved back to Dublin, we took it with us and planted it in front of the kitchen window. I'm practical enough to know that the perfect white roses it produces all year round while every other plant in the garden struggles for survival are purely coincidental, but I'm pleased that it thrives.

But it's a rose bush, not a baby. And when I see my three perfect children play around it, I know there should be four of them, that once there were. There are whole days that pass now without me thinking about him, but they aren't many. Most days, I think about who he might have been, this little person who we never met, who we never named, whose gender we never knew. And I remember his heartbeat on a screen, a little piston that stopped short, and it still makes me cry. Because however briefly, I was his mother.

TEETHING TROUBLES

SMALL GIRL: 6 YEARS, 7 MONTHS
BOY: 4 YEARS, 6 MONTHS
BABY: 2 YEARS, 1 MONTH

All of a sudden, The Small Girl has no front teeth. Too late to tie in with the seasonal song, the first of her top teeth departed seconds after she met a disappointing Santa Claus at Santa's Kingdom, and under the circumstances, you couldn't blame it. After that, the remaining baby tooth relaxed into its more spacious surroundings and actually shifted into the centre of the gap, where it dangled precariously for three weeks. It clung on like a wobbling tombstone while The Small Girl prayed for a big miracle, one that would allow her new tooth to grow to full size before its neighbour finally gave up the ghost.

But even as the pine needles began softly to hit the floor last weekend, the last tooth knew its goose was cooked. On Saturday afternoon, I attacked an epic pile of ironing while watching *Airport 79: The Concorde* (the only film I got to see over Christmas: how sad is that?), while The Toddler dozed on the couch, The Boy made some unpleasant noises with a Power Ranger and The Small Girl and her best friend discussed world events from the perspective of the under-sevens. Then, suddenly, just as the co-pilot delivered the immortal line, 'The Alps! Straight ahead!' gravity finally prevailed. The Small Girl screamed, feeling blood in her mouth for the first time (the three predecessors had been quick and clean), The Boy burst into hysterical sobs about how lucky his sister was – he alone thinking ahead to the financial pay-off – The Best Friend embarked on a story about how all of this was as nothing compared to what had befallen her earlier in the day, when her 'ear was gushing', The Toddler woke up and fell off the couch and Concorde crashed into the mountain.

Ten minutes later we all (apart from the passengers on the stricken Concorde) had a celebratory treat and toasted a future of permanent teeth. All of us, that is, except The Small Girl, who'd taken to her bed to lament her altered appearance. It took half an hour of reassurance, coaxing and tears (why do I always cry at these miniature milestones?) to convince her that losing this last front tooth was a positive development and that no, she didn't look stupid.

And it was true. There is something peculiar about this toothless time that allows six-year-olds to wander around with gummy smiles without anyone even noticing. A three-year-old without their front teeth will always turn heads, as will a nine-year-old, yet for some merciful reason we don't even notice whether kids in the tooth-losing age range are with or without.

We also seem to have little memory of our own gumminess. I can recall every single detail of my childhood (which is just as well, since the greater part of my adult life is a blur), but I can barely remember losing my baby teeth and I have no real sense of how it felt to have no front teeth at all. The only clear memory associated with the whole baby tooth business is of losing one of my front teeth to a crème egg as I was walking down the road with my sister, singing 'Does Your Chewing Gum Lose Its Flavour on the Bed Post Over Night'. It was a thoroughly unpleasant experience – and that was before the tooth fell out. The subsequent sight of it drowning slowly in a blood-streaked yellowy fondant is one that stayed with me for a long time and effectively turned me off crème eggs for years. (I returned to them briefly in my late teens until somebody told me that there were more calories in a single crème egg than in an entire sliced pan. I've no idea whether that's true or not, but crème eggs and I have been strangers since.)

I also seem to recall that the going rate for a tooth back then was fifty pence, which probably means that today's children are being short-changed by the tooth fairy. The first time that generous little soul visited our house was when The Boy lost his front tooth in a terrible accident, and, being both traumatised by the experience and a little drunk, the fairy left a load of money and a gift. The Small Girl was warned that by the time her teeth started to fall, routine and sobriety would probably have returned and so a rate of €2 per tooth was established. Last Saturday, since there was blood and tears, the fairy increased its payment by a euro, and there was universal rejoicing as a result.

In fact, the only shadow on the sunny morning that followed that dog-day afternoon came from the fairy's representative who suddenly realised that she had absolutely no idea what she'd done with the five teeth that have now been extracted from under pillows in this house. Other parents keep their children's first teeth and lay them on tiny cushions in hand-crafted receptacles; all our receptacles remain empty, which can only mean that somewhere out there, there are five tiny time-bombs just waiting to trip us up. My only hope is that by the time they are eventually uncovered, we will have a house full of adult teeth to smile at the innocence of it all. And if I could still have all my own teeth, my own hair and most of my marbles, then we might even have another celebratory treat. Probably not a crème egg, though: if you have managed to keep your own teeth long after your children have stopped losing theirs, you really shouldn't tempt fate.

DAYS LIKE THESE

SMALL GIRL: 6 YEARS,10 MONTHS
BOY: 4 YEARS, 9 MONTHS
TODDLER: 2 YEARS, 4 MONTHS

The Small Girl has lost her best friend. It has been a painful and protracted break-up, complicated by an exchange of unpleasant-ries that I am way too ashamed to go into here. Suffice to say that there are a number of people round these parts who don't feel particularly proud of themselves at the moment, and I am firmly amongst them.

But these girls were no fairweather, five-minute friends. They were sealed and bonded for a full quarter of their young lives – so much so that six months ago, The Small Girl cheerfully informed her elderly English grandmother that she was gay. 'I thought we'd be best friends when we were seventy,' she sobbed when the hatchet fell, and I have to admit I'd thought so as well. Having overheard them plan their First Communions, their nights out as teenagers, their weddings and their children's names together, I too had thought it was the real deal, and I can honestly say I've been more upset by their parting than I ever was about the end of one of my own relationships. Which, in one way, just goes to show how shallow I am. But my daughter has suddenly lost a little bit of her sparkle and even though she is a child who could have bottled and sold sparkle without ever missing any, it still hurts.

In the middle of all of this, The Boy has been thrown out of the diminutive gang that hangs around the green at the end of the road. His ejection, several short people called at the door to tell us, came as a result of his ferocious bad language and his overzealous use of the light-sabre. And just to put the Smartie on the cake, I have suddenly noticed that The Toddler has developed a huge and horrific-looking bald spot on her scalp, the result of her constantly twisting strands of her lovely blonde hair around her fingers. The Book says she might be stressed. I know how she feels. Nobody told me there'd be days like this.

And on days like these, you sometimes wonder what life would be like if you'd taken the road less travelled. If I hadn't been a hormonally-driven, biological clock-watching lunatic, I would be up-to-date on matters cinematic and theatrical. I could watch videos in the afternoon. I would have heard the Katie Melua album. I would have read every Booker short-listed novel of the past five years and I would have at least attempted to have one of my own included on that noble list. I would read newspapers on the day they're published.

We would go on holidays that didn't include airport transfers and entertainment co-ordinators. We might have been to Asia. We would lose count of how many weekends away we'd had. Sometimes, we would have sex without the covers on. We would go out on a whim without having to put a raft of contingency plans into action. We would go to nightclubs and we wouldn't always have to leave them early in order to get back to the babysitter. We would eat out regularly, and my passion for cooking wouldn't have got stuck somewhere in the mid-1990s, along the Pacific Rim. I wouldn't always know what's for dinner, days in advance. I could have lunch and stay out until well after teatime.

In the gym, I wouldn't have to kill myself trying to complete my programme in an hour so that I could collect The Toddler from the crèche. I could take a sauna. When that knot of tension forms between my shoulder blades, I could have a massage instead of taking two paracetemol. I wouldn't get that knot of tension between my shoulder blades. I would still have long nails. I would have breasts instead of diddies. I could take a bath instead of a shower and stay in it till my fingers wrinkled. I could go to the shops without having to pack. I could try on clothes in shops instead of panic-buying everything and returning the majority of it afterwards. I wouldn't need to use the washing machine every day.

I could go and see The Hoops more than a couple of times each season and I might even go to away games. I could go to the European Championships. I could walk the pier without worrying that somebody would fall in.

I wouldn't have seen all my contemporaries promoted ahead of me. I wouldn't have to work nights. I would have fragile ornaments instead of Buzz Lightyear on my Habitat shelves. I would live somewhere trendy. I wouldn't look my age. My body wouldn't force me out of bed at seven on a Saturday and Sunday morning. Nobody else's would either. I would never, ever have to drive. I wouldn't have life insurance. I wouldn't be in the VHI. If I died, it wouldn't ruin anyone else's life.

And then, you look out the window and you happen to see somebody who's been waiting outside the house for a whole hour for an ice-cream van that mightn't have ever come, and you're lucky enough to catch her buying her very first 99, all by herself. And when she runs in she's beaming with pride and a little bit of her sparkle is back. And later on, a pair of pudgy, sticky arms wrap themselves around you, and a warm little face buries itself in your neck and from somewhere in between that matted, no-longer-to-be-brushed hair, the stale ice-cream and the warm flesh, a little voice contentedly purrs, 'My Mammy'. And even on days like these, there's no contest.

LENT

SMALL GIRL: 6 YEARS, 10 MONTHS
BOY: 4 YEARS, 9 MONTHS
TODDLER: 2 YEARS, 4 MONTHS

This week, I will be mostly eating chocolate. Having spent the last forty days wandering in a confectionery desert – which also, for the record, was devoid of crisps and biscuits – I think I have earned the right to eat myself egg-shaped. Under the circumstances, it would seem churlish not to.

If it is any consolation, I will not take (much) pleasure in it. One of the more disturbing aspects of my character is my utter inability to see food – good, bad or indifferent – go to waste, and so I will be obliged this week, sure as sugar, to hoover up all those broken bits of Easter egg that the smaller mouths in the house have rejected. Half-eaten soft-centre, anyone? Buttons that have been left too close to the radiator and have merged into a single chocolatey mess? Come one, come all, I say.

Of course, I'm writing this on a promise, as it were. Back here, we are still in the dwindling days of Lent, those last few hours of abstinence where small people start asking what a difference a day makes and grown-ups aren't entirely sure of the answer. The prolonged school holiday doesn't help, of course; my kids equate the words 'school's out' with 'treats in' and persuading them to at least wait until they've laid Christ in the tomb is akin to rolling away the stone myself.

Actually, the whole Easter story has taken on a new life in our home this year and I'm not at all sure that I'm spinning it right. The

Small Girl is going through a deeply philosophical phase and spends long periods wondering where exactly heaven is and why nobody on a plane or a spaceship has ever seen it. She's also been reflecting on the very nature of God and asking pertinent questions about his motives. Her stock response to my laboured ones is to pronounce happily that whatever I've just said is 'completely mad' or just plain 'weird'. Still, she got to bring up the gifts on Holy Thursday, and as long as the perks keep coming, we may get her to her First Communion in a state of grace yet.

She gave up chocolate biscuits, by the way, and made up for it by munching her way through chocolate chip cookies for all of Lent, which, when you're six, is probably permissible. At thirty-seven, though, a little more was required, and so my own sugar famine was entire and is almost complete. I also managed to give up weighing myself for the duration, which may not sound like much of a sacrifice, but when you weigh yourself twice a day (oh yes), it's quite a trial. I also – and I need to be careful here, given that I'm still in a Lenten position – gave up talking about my weight. In that, I confess to a single lapse, which came about as a result of a new pair of trousers and an absolute compulsion to ask The Husband if my bum looked big in them. As several crap country singers have said before me, I'm only human, I'm just a woman.

I sometimes wish there was something a little more worthy or grandiose for grown-ups to do in Lent but when you're shackled by small penitents, it's hard to be humble or any of those other virtues Lent should bring in abundance. If I had gone to Mass every day in the company of three small jiggly children I might have unwittingly caused other people to give up their religion, and likewise, if we'd frequented the elderly or the housebound, something terrible might have happened.

In any event, good living can mean you happen across bad people. My two sisters and I were once mugged on our way back from an Easter vigil, which always struck me as very poor timing on everyone's part. It's the kind of statistic The Small Girl might even declare 'completely mad'. Still, at least we were in a position to forgive our assailants.

Actually, we were able to do more than that. About a year afterwards, I was half-watching 'Garda Patrol' while doing the ironing when I heard a description of a suspect in an armed robbery and recognised it as the youth who'd almost torn my arm from my socket an Easter ago. I rang the number given and passed on my information to a Garda who couldn't have been either less interested or less polite. If anything, he just sounded a bit suspicious. The next time I was mugged, the Gardaí appeared to take it a bit more seriously and spent quite a long time trying to persuade me to identify a man they assured me was the one who'd attacked me. In the end, I declined. And about a year later, at a party, I happened to meet the Garda who'd interviewed me. That was the man, he told me, and he was now in prison, having admitted to about eighty crimes, my own little contretemps among them. And to put the chocolate icing on the cake, he told me, they'd all had a great laugh down at the station over my name.

I've no idea why I'm telling you all this. I need sugar and I need it now.

TICKLING STICK

SMALL GIRL: 6 YEARS, 11 MONTHS
BOY: 4 YEARS, 10 MONTHS
TODDLER: 2 YEARS, 5 MONTHS

The Toddler has just learnt life's most depressing lesson: you can't tickle yourself. No doubt, there will be other disappointments down the road but none will ever tell her more about the wretchedness of the world than the one she's just experienced. Life is unfair and the world is a terrible place if you can't even cheer yourself up with a bit of a tickle.

And God knows, she tried. Liberated at last from baby vests that fasten underneath a nappy, she suddenly has access to her own tummy, her lovely, round, soft tummy that just begs to be tickled. She gave it her best shot, rolling her little vest all the way up and letting her hand scrabble across her flesh. She even made that high-pitched 'tickly tickly' sound. But it was to no avail. What made it worse was the fact that I reached over in the middle of her exertions and just touched her tummy with my fingertip, and suddenly she was in creases. Thus inspired, she tried just tipping herself as I had done, and then looked at me in puzzled sadness when nothing happened. I tried to console her but her disappointed face said that she's just realised it's all downhill from here.

The human body might be a truly miraculous entity, capable of eating and sleeping and loving and hating, but it cannot give itself a good laugh. Others might find your body hilarious, but unless you have an almost mystical sense of detachment, it cannot do it for you. The Toddler, just past two, suddenly understands this and it is a terrible truth. If she weren't her mother's daughter, it might be enough to put her off her food.

To be honest, I don't quite get it either. Wouldn't the world be a brighter place if we could tickle ourselves? Would Osama be so mean if he spent just five minutes a day scratching under his beard and chortling accordingly? Would David Beckham have turned to Rebecca Loos if he could have overcome his loneliness by tickling his six-pack? Would we need psychiatrists or counsellors, courts or prisons if we all possessed the ability to lift our moods and make ourselves laugh like monkeys at the drop of a hat? Would funerals be so sad?

I realise that it might just be me, The Toddler and Ken Dodd on this one, but the fact is that there are so many people who you just know would be really, really good at it. (Ironically, I suspect Ken Dodd mightn't actually be one of them, but I have a feeling that he may have enough to deal with on a day-to-day basis without having to worry about scheduling a tickling session.) But Bertie looks as though he were built for self-tickling and I'll wager Paidí O'Sé would be a less complex character if he were given free rein over his ribs. I don't think that Dolores O'Riordan would be much good at it but since she's such a wonderful mother, she probably wouldn't need it as much as the rest of us.

I know that there is a neurological explanation as to why we can't tickle ourselves – believe it or not, I care enough about this outrage to have checked out the logistics of it before – but frankly, that's not good enough. We can grow ears on mice and conjure sheep out of thin air, so why has nobody spent any time trying to fix the tickling thing? Given that the therapeutic and healing properties of laughter have been scientifically established, wouldn't boffins be better occupied concentrating on forwarding the cause of self-tickling instead of trying to grow human organs in test tubes? Would we need organ donation at all if we all enjoyed a daily tickle?

We could, of course, just tickle each other, but that raises all manner of difficulties. Some people might discover that there is nobody to tickle them, others might complain about their tickler's technique. Also, there is a fine line between tickle and assault, and the courts might soon be filled with frivolous lawsuits regarding unsatisfactory tickling. Besides, as a general rule, all good ideas have already been thought of, and if formation tickling by strangers was the way forward, it would have been legislated for by now.

There are other mysteries perplexing The Toddler at the moment, chief amongst them is why it is socially unacceptable to urinate on the floor. I have to say that on this one, I part company with her. I would even go so far as to say that if we all pissed on the floor, then Osama would be meaner, Beckham would be lonelier, Bertie would be an embarrassment and Paidí's pub would be a health hazard. Funnily enough, I've no difficulty with Dolores O'Riordan urinating all over the place on the basis that she seems to have loads of people around her who would be willing to clean it up.

So they're the lessons learnt by the unfortunate Toddler this week. Up until now, it's been balls, bottles, balloons and Balamory all the way, and now, suddenly, she's discovered that she can't tickle herself and she has to use the toilet. Sometimes I wonder, when we promised her it would be a wonderful world, if we mightn't have sold her a pup.

UNTRENDY MOTHER

SMALL GIRL: 6 YEARS, 11 MONTHS
BOY: 4 YEARS, 10 MONTHS
TODDLER: 2 YEARS, 5 MONTHS

I have suddenly plunged so far down in my children's estimation that I am in danger of suffering credibility bends. Six weeks ago, they regarded me as some sort of foul-mouthed Mary Poppins, if you can imagine such a thing – now, they are looking at me in the way you might size up a mad relative for a berth in the attic. Insofar as parents exist to embarrass their children, I always knew it would happen: I just never expected it to be so damned *efficient*.

It started a couple of weeks back, when I went to rendezvous with The Small Girl after school. Being within stretching distance of seven, she now walks up the road by herself, while I simply show up at journey's end to steward her across the main road. Usually, I'm there before she is – partly for the sport of watching her tiny frame bounce up the road beneath a giant schoolbag while passers-by wonder what kind of negligent mother the poor infant has. On this occasion, though, she beat me to it. As I rounded the corner and saw her already in place, I broke into what I thought was a modest canter but what, to her, clearly resembled some sort of forward-moving epileptic attack. Even from twenty yards away, I could see her raise her eyebrows to heaven. Her first words, as soon as she'd executed the road, were 'You look like a geek.' This was swiftly followed by an explanation of how it's bad enough being the smallest girl in the whole school (which is an exaggeration; there are some junior infants smaller) without having a mother who insists on running in four-inch heels.

At least, I consoled myself, The Boy still thinks the sun shines out of my backside. But it quickly turned out that he too has seen the light and realised that it's coming from another direction entirely. Until a whistle ago, the only aspect of my inglorious career that impressed my children was the fact that I once worked with Dustin. The evidence of the association is a DVD that is occasionally viewed, though seldom requested. It has become, if you like, the DVD of Peace – popped in when the older two can't agree on their Saturday evening's entertainment.

Anyway, it was in this compromise role that 'Dustin's Fowl Play' – lovingly scripted by my own fair hand – enjoyed an airing last weekend. And initially, it seemed to work a treat: perfect peace ensued while The Husband and I enjoyed a meal in the other room. It was only as I crept past the living-room door en route to the smallest room that I overheard the grim reality within. 'This is CRAP!' came The Boy's voice. I hovered; he hesitated. Then, even more emphatically, 'Jesus wept!' If it had been a phrase either myself or The Husband frequented, it mightn't have been so bad. But there it was, my professional life condemned with a phrase specially imported from the road by a four-year-old. Jesus wept.

But the final nail was driven – again – by his older sister. There she was, cute as a button, snuggling up to her dad while he helped her draw Scooby Doo. Now The Husband, it should be said, is a bit of an artist and so is always drafted in for the nuances of character drawing. And apparently, he is much admired. 'Dad, you're so good at drawing,' she purred. And while she was down there, 'And you're really good at music as well. You're great at everything.'

It's my own fault, of course. I should have just let it lie, a beautiful daddy/daughter moment. But no. My confidence was already dented and perhaps I craved approval from miniature mouths. And what am I good at? I ventured. In fairness, she gave the question a great deal of consideration. Too much, perhaps – Jeremy Paxman would have offered it to the other team long before the answer was delivered. But then it came, the thing that I am really, really good at: 'eating very fast.'

It could be worse, of course, and depressingly, it will get much, much worse. My best friend's ten-year-old daughter lives her life in a perpetual state of mortification over her father. His crimes, to most grown-up minds, are minimal: a couple of poor choices of outfit and a penchant for wearing his Celtic slippers at the end of the evening. Her friend, meanwhile, can't even bring herself to look at her embarrassment of a father, who has disgraced himself by being useful on the guitar and enjoying traditional music. I seem to remember that there was a girl in my class in primary school who almost died of shame over her mother's pencilled-on eyebrows – or maybe that was just the rest of us, embarrassed on her behalf.

Either way, the rules of parenthood are elusive and unbelievably complex. Thou shalt not run in high heels or wear Celtic slippers. Don't pencil in a joke or pencil on your eyebrows. Only play the guitar if you can do a Busted number, unless your daughter is over ten, in which case playing a Busted number is punishable by ten years of sullen silence, which will only be broken when the daughter needs the deposit on a house. Even then, only visit it when invited and don't offer any advice on décor lest you want to be the brunt of a hundred dinner party anecdotes. Finally, accept that where kids are concerned, you simply can't win. Even when you really hoped the fight might last a few more rounds.

RABBIT RABBIT

SMALL GIRL: 7 YEARS
BOY: 4 YEARS, 11 MONTHS
TODDLER: 2 YEARS, 6 MONTHS

A quick joke: a rabbit runs into a butcher's shop and says, 'Have you got any cabbages?' Butcher replies, 'No, sorry, this is a butcher's shop.' Next day, the rabbit comes into the shop again. 'Have you got any cabbages?' Vexed butcher replies that he told the rabbit yesterday, they don't sell cabbages. Next day, rabbit runs in again. 'Have you got any cabbages?' Butcher: 'Look, if you ever come into this shop again asking for cabbages, I'll nail your bloody long ears to the floor.' Next day, rabbit runs in again. 'Have you got any nails?' 'No,' says the confused butcher. Rabbit: 'Have you got any cabbages?'

Anyway, for the last couple of weeks, I've been living a sort of lopsided, lop-eared version of that joke. I have rung up every purveyor of pets in south Dublin with what I originally thought was a simple request: 'Have you got any rabbits?' It turns out, though, that in spite of their legendary reputation in the bedroom department, rabbits are elusive creatures at the customer's end of the retail chain. They seem to be permanently on the way in, just run out or expected Tuesday. Tuesday never really comes, though, as 'the man' doesn't come in when he's supposed to and now the shopkeeper can't really say when or indeed if he'll ever have rabbits again. One pet shop owner cheerfully told me, 'We never know when we'll have them. We don't know when a litter is going to be born.' My understanding was that there's one born every minute, but if there are, then they are living out their short, glorious lives in another part of the world. 'They go very fast,' the same shopkeeper assured me. 'The best thing you can do is phone me every day.'

I didn't quite share that view and in the end, I didn't have to. In another pet shop, Tuesday finally arrived last Saturday and the man showed up. My daily phone call confirmed that finally, there be rabbits, so we loaded the kids in the car, picked up an empty Pampers box and headed off to expand our family. Just before we left the house, I ran upstairs and pulled a soft, well-worn carrycot sheet from the hot press and put it in the box. I'm sure there was something deeply significant about that and one day I'll have to deal with it. Last Saturday, though, there was no time. I was too afraid they would go very fast.

We have been under immense pressure for ages on the pet front. Recently, it has come to the stage that the kids are more or less stopping strangers in shops to tell them, mournfully, that they have no pet. Their sad admission is usually accompanied by an accusing glance at the perpetrator of this petless state, who smiles apologetically and says, by way of compensation, 'Have you got any cabbages?' Of course, there was a bigger villain than I in all of this, even if I shouldered all the blame. However much I didn't want a pet, The Husband was dead set against any further dependents and it took several carrots on sticks to persuade him otherwise.

And in the process, I somehow managed to convince myself as well. Once we'd moved away from dogs – too smelly, way too much hard work, would eat the Habitat sofa – and cats – I'm happily allergic – the idea of a little creature became increasingly appealing with every damning look from the petless generation. I may have told you that we had a guinea pig when I was a child.

Then we had two and then, because I couldn't bear to give them away, suddenly we had seventy-six. Long before that point, it was made clear to me that if I couldn't let go, then I would have to become sole custodian and cleaner to the collection. So, while other people spent their adolescence being ridden by angst, I passed mine shovelling seventy-six guinea pigs' shit twice a week. Those were happy days in so many ways in the garage I knew so well.

I'd have gone the guinea-pig road again, but in the absence of a garage we have been forced to go for an outdoor type. So a rabbit it was, and a rabbit it is. As the kids ran up to the cage in the pet shop and shouted out 'I want that one' with three fingers indicating three different bunnies, it looked like we had chosen a hard road, but just minutes later, the two older ones sought us out in the hutch department and, hand in hand, told us they'd made a decision. And so the newest member of our family was chosen.

The Small Girl wanted to call him Paul, which seemed like a very sensible name for a rabbit, but since we don't yet know his gender, we decided to opt for a more ambiguous name. The Husband wanted Pat, for political reasons, and I liked Starsky, for comedic ones. In the end, we agreed on Coinín. He is brown and tiny and a thing of joy and a magnet for every small child in the area. And in spite of his hardiness, he has yet to spend a night outdoors. He's very young, see, and he has this carrycot blanket thing that he seems to like. As I said, there may well be issues here.

SCHOOLBOY

SMALL GIRL: 7 YEARS, 3 MONTHS
BOY: 5 YEARS, 2 MONTHS
TODDLER: 2 YEARS, 9 MONTHS

Somewhat predictably, The Boy crashed his bike into a tree two days before he started school and so he embarked on formal education with facial injuries he himself described as 'disgusting'. It only occurred to me as I walked back home from the school that the combination of his impressive height – some of the boys in his class are literally up to his elbow – and his disgusting face may have prompted some of his new colleagues to form the completely erroneous view that The Boy is, in some way, hard. I can only speculate that we may have to deal with the results of that presumption – possibly through the court system – in the years ahead.

More immediately, his injuries meant that we left the camera at home on the milestone first day. I hope, in years to come, we remember why the first pictures of this new schoolboy were taken a week late – when he'd already developed the weariness of the lifer and the shirt-hanging-out attitude that goes along with it. If we don't recall the disgusting face, the disgusted Boy might conclude that because he is a middle child, we simply didn't bother.

I know that was the conclusion I came to when I made my Confirmation and nobody bothered recording any aspect of the occasion photographically. And I still blame Middle Child Syndrome by proxy for the fact that my whole family managed to go on holidays without me when I was about six, and nobody missed me until they were on the Naas dual carriageway. In fact, pretty much everything that hasn't gone my way up until this point could be put down to Middle Child Syndrome, now recognised by the bearded professions as a genuine affliction.

But coming from the other side of it, there is no doubt that the second child's first day at school lacks the emotion and the wrench of the first. I love a decent wallow, as it happens, and I'd have been quite happy to have fetched up at the Parents' Association Tea and Sympathy stall in tears, but on the day, I just couldn't muster the mood. Perhaps it was the two years of playschool already tucked under his belt, or the fact that he looked as though he'd got waylaid on the way to third class, but it just wasn't the same. The lump in the throat that accompanied The Small Girl's first day never materialised and the only real sense of wonder concerned how, using the same gene pool, we have managed to produce a child who is the biggest in his class and one who is the smallest.

I reserve the right to fall asunder when The Toddler starts and the nest really empties out – but in the meantime, I'm afraid The Boy's big day out failed to tug the eager heartstrings. For his part, he played with stickle bricks, coloured in 'a really big muffin' and announced in the evening that he would only be going on occasional days from now on. It took The Husband's gentle but firm suggestion that he get out and get a job to make him change his mind. Cue the weariness and the shirt-sticking-out-thing.

But there was plenty of emotion still to spill out on that awful day and in the days that followed it. Even as The Boy was happily colouring his really big muffin, the children of Beslan Number One school were embarking on a tragic journey the scale of which is still almost unimaginable. Three years ago, The Small Girl started school on the same day as those awful scenes at Holy Cross Primary in the Ardoyne; I remember then contrasting her happy experience with the brutality those four-year-olds faced on their first day at school. Then, it was the hair that seemed to me the poignant image: little girls with tears of terror streaming down their faces and beautiful, lovingly-placed new ribbons in their perfect hair in anticipation of their glorious adventure ahead.

I noticed it again on Friday, children running for their lives in their underwear but still, even after three days of hell, with their new hair clips and ribbons in place. Comparisons end there. It is impossible to contrast The Boy's debut in school with what happened in Beslan because the two events barely belong in the same world. All I understand is that on Friday evening, at the end of his first week in school, I held my boy tight and thanked everything for really big muffins, shirts sticking out and superficial disgusting facial injuries.

We live in a shocking, terrifying world, but we are blessed beyond belief that our little piece of it remains a sanctuary of bumped knees and *an-bhfuil-cead-agam-dul-amach*. And if that is insular and selfish, then so be it. But when your own children stand proudly in front of you for the first time in brand new school uniforms, then the bigger picture and the big bad world are sometimes too terrible to countenance.

BREAD HEAD

SMALL GIRL: 7 YEARS, 3 MONTHS
BOY: 5 YEARS, 2 MONTHS
TODDLER: 2 YEARS, 9 MONTHS

The Small Girl has become a bread head. Having paced out the first seven years of her life with neither an interest in nor any significant understanding of money – for her, every day was a Buy Nothing Day – she has suddenly become the Gordon Gecko of the primary-school circuit. Her extraordinary descent into capitalism – at a time when she's till struggling with capital letters – can be traced entirely to one single change in her little life: she is allowed to go to the shops on her own.

To say that this has changed her world is an epic understatement. Learning to walk didn't have as profound an impact on her movements as being allowed to walk, unaided, the 200 metres or so down to the local shops. Suddenly, money makes her world go around and the spending of it has become her life's work.

Even her long-term ambitions have been adjusted accordingly. Having declared, since she knew the words, that she would be a pop star when she grew up, she's now revised the career plan and announced that she will be a pop star first, and then she will work in a shop. Like Hear'Say, The Husband offered.

By a happy coincidence, her teeth are tumbling out like there's no tomorrow, and so the tooth fairies are providing a steady source of income. I suspect she is actually pulling them out herself now, so consuming is her desire to collect and dispatch wealth. And the fairies, I also suspect, are not her sole benefactors. By my calculations, she can't have accrued more than €15 on the tooth front, yet she seems to have a never-ending supply of cash. I can only conclude that members of my own family are feeding her habit when I'm not looking. If that is the case, I can only regret that such nefarious practices were not in place when I was growing up.

In fairness to her, it is not all me, me, me. She is more than happy to buy treats for her younger siblings and if there is a slight imbalance between hers and theirs on the quality and quantity front, none of them seems to mind too much. In fact, the only people who are possibly put out by this development are the women working in the shop. They must dread her arrival, given that she has a peculiar habit of buying just one thing at a time, even when she has several items on her wish list. She does it, she tells me, so she can keep track of her spending. Perhaps she is her mother's daughter after all. She's also offered to pay for the occasional messages that I send her for and while I've thus far graciously refused, it's a personality trait I'm very much hoping will still be evident when she is over eighteen and old enough to buy her poor mammy drink. In the meantime, I have to settle for slightly more mundane grand gestures.

The grandest of all came last week when a little bird (that may or may not have borne a striking resemblance to me) advised her that her mother's birthday was cantering around the corner. In spite of my protestations, she insisted that she would buy me a birthday present and canvassed my opinion on what I'd like. Undeterred by my Irish Mammy-style 'ah, no, I'll be fine, sure what would I need with things' reply, she thought long and hard before landing on what she clearly believed was the winner. 'I know,' she announced, 'would you like something that would help you make the lunches faster?'

Even as I agreed that this would be a dream come true, I was back in the hardware shop down the road, a seven-year-old bread head myself, choosing a present for my own unfortunate mother's birthday. I can still remember how I went down there four or five times on reconnaissance missions before I finally settled on a magnificent floor cloth for the birthday girl. It cost thirty pence and I can still see the two women who worked there absolutely breaking their arses laughing when I told them it was a birthday present for my mother. For all their scorn, I went home and wrapped it up, then hid it away until the great day. An hour later, I could wait for the great day no longer and I handed the present over to a hugely impressed and grateful mother, whose birthday fell in April. It was February.

Anyway, somewhere between intent and invention, my own gadget to speed up the lunch-making process fell. Maybe she finally ran out of money or maybe, like her mother, she just couldn't think how the whole business could be more efficiently run. Whatever happened, I ended up with a slightly alarming looking and not entirely practical mask, a homemade present that she worked on for hours every day for a whole week before the grand occasion. It is perfect, on the basis that homemade presents are the best sort when your children are under ten. After that, I give fair notice now, don't even think about it. If my kids are going to go down a road where greed is good, then the least I should demand is a cut of the profits.

PLAYGROUP BLUES

SMALL GIRL: 7 YEARS, 4 MONTHS
BOY: 5 YEARS, 3 MONTHS
YOUNGEST: 2 YEARS, 10 MONTHS

The Toddler has started playschool, which probably means she now deserves to be promoted to Youngest. It also possibly qualifies us both for a bed in the local puzzle factory. That it hasn't been a textbook start for either of us is an understatement.

In fairness, the omens hadn't been good. After an entire summer where she answered every question with a triumphant cry of 'The Rainbow School!' – thus facilitating fascinating exchanges like 'What do you want for your dinner?' – 'The Rainbow School!' – the pot of preschool gold dulled considerably in the past few weeks, to the extent that, by D-day, she was so twisted with anxiety and worry that she appeared to have had a perm. At least she wasn't suffering alone. Having been convinced for a whole year that she was ready for this first step into education, I spent the last few nights watching her sleep, still in night-time nappies, still in a cot, still sucking on her soother with a ferocity that makes her soft, protruding tummy palpitate all on its own. Sweet Jesus, she's still a baby. And here I was, Cruella de Ville, sending her down the playschool mine. For shame.

So it was no great surprise that we both ended up in tears on the first day. And while it was far worse for her – she really only let up to breathe – it cut even deeper into my wretched heart, especially when she raised her pudgy arms to me and, between sobs, wailed the awful words, 'I need you'.

(I'll leave the grief trough for a moment to pass on a parenting tip to anyone out there who's in the market: never teach a child the word 'need'. There is no usage which will make you happy; in most contexts, it will drive you to despair – 'I need Coco Pops', 'I need another wee' – and in some – 'I need you' – it can kill you.) Eventually, the teacher, who's already been around the block with me, threw me out. When The Boy was a student of life and recreation, I couldn't wait to put clear concrete between me and the Rainbow School every morning, but he didn't have pleady, needy eyes and, crucially, he wasn't my baby. If there is a league table of sanity in pre-school mothers, then last Monday I dropped two whole divisions.

When I went back to collect her, I did so with a screwed-on grin and a pair of open arms. She didn't so much run into them as stagger, her little body still racked with sobs. Then, before I could utter a word, she announced 'that was a lovely day', before falling apart all over again.

Clearly convinced that the Rainbow School was now behind her, she slept her perfect baby sleep that night while I got the regulation hour-and-a-half's slumber of the guilty mother. In the morning, we had another wrestling match on the threshold of the playschool before I abandoned her all over again. Too early and too upset for the editorial meeting (yes, we have them), I walked around Stephen's Green for half an hour in tears and, as is the way of these things, I met everyone I've ever known, all out for the day to witness my shame.

Back home, on that darkest day, The Youngest, my baby, decided to have nothing further to do with me. Summoning up every ounce of guile two years and ten months of a hard life can afford you, she spent the afternoon ignoring me, snubbing me and downright spiting me. If you weren't me, it was almost comical – I've rarely seen my parents enjoying themselves more without a carvery being present – but for the mother who sent The Toddler away, it was hell. Eventually, she decided she needed to make a jigsaw more urgently than make a point and an entente of sorts emerged.

That was the worst day. After a third morning of the kind of scenes traditionally only observed on railway-station platforms, the sainted teacher suggested The Husband bring her instead. He did, and she waved him off happily and by the end of the first week, she had gone a whole morning without a single sob.

When I collected her on the second Monday, she jumped into my arms without an agenda and volunteered that she had had 'a nice time'. Somehow, as the tears have dried up, so have the night-time nappies. And yesterday she took me aside for a quiet word about how she really needs a 'big girl's bed.'

She does, too. I have kept her in the cot way too long, partly for my own emotional reasons but also because, without a usurper teething at her heels, she's been so content to be a baby. Now she's decided to move up in to the world, and I've only myself to blame. She will, of course, be just fine. I wish I could be as bullish about myself. But as I stand in an empty kitchen gazing out the window, I can't help thinking that the only thing standing between me and a straitjacket is the fact that there is no pre-school for pet rabbits. I just hope he likes his new cot.

HALLOWE'EN

SMALL GIRL: 7 YEARS, 4 MONTHS
BOY: 5 YEARS, 3 MONTHS
YOUNGEST: 2 YEARS, 10 MONTHS

The Youngest has decided to boycott Hallowe'en. There has been a residual protest going on for weeks concerning our weekend away in Inchydoney – for the duration of which she was cruelly cast into the care of her overly-indulgent aunt – and I still haven't been entirely forgiven for heartlessly sending her to playschool, but whether these injustices have directly led her to this day of (in)action isn't entirely apparent. Whatever her motives, the result is clear: we are one down for the serious business of tricking and treating tonight.

Her intentions were flagged more that a fortnight ago, even before the Hallowe'en decorations appeared in the shops to compete for attention with the Christmas favours. 'I hate Hallowe'en,' she announced, and she has been emphatic ever since. Prevailed upon to elaborate, she will only volunteer that the whole thing is 'too horrible'. Even the steady arrival in the house this week of balloons, garlands and pumpkins hasn't turned her head. As to dressing up, she won't so much as view the costume options available – and as the youngest child on the entire road, she has a pretty impressive range to choose from. I seem to remember my childhood Hallowe'ens consisted largely of an annual fight between myself and my sisters over who got to wear my mother's wedding dress. The losers, as far as I recall, got to wear their own clothes and sulk while watching television in Irish for the evening (why did RTÉ do that? Was the occasion not scary enough?). If we'd had the cats and witches and princesses and pirates so readily rejected by The Youngest this week, we might be all living on the Vico Road by now.

But it's not just in the costume department that she's revolting. All last week, the older two were gleefully drip-feeding paintings of pumpkins and mosaics of monsters into the Hallowe'en party, as the school made serious inroads into the national reserves of orange and black paint. Back at the Rainbow Playschool, I was quietly notified by the authorities that The Youngest had steadfastly refused to involve herself in any such nonsense, and that all efforts to persuade her painted pumpkin-wards had failed. On the last day before the mid-term, I watched all the other children run out to their mothers behind masks, messes and rough representations of things that go bump in the night, while my own happily emerged with her face shining and her arms swinging. In the local shop, while her fellow pre-schoolers ran around like devilish dervishes, she conceded to admire a particularly fat pumpkin suspended from the ceiling. 'But you hate Hallowe'en,' I pounced, thinking the matter about to be settled in my favour. 'Oh yes,' she remembered, and refused to look ceiling-ward for the rest of the week.

Of course, it may be a protest over the gross commercialisation of the festival and if it is, then it's an admirable stand. I too deplore the manner in which we have so eagerly embraced the American version of a festival that is wholly Irish, and I long for simpler times when kids traipsed around the roads dressed in bin liners and their mothers' shoes and were glad to get a monkey nut for their trouble. Back then, expectations were shockingly low and standards happily rowed in accordingly.

Now, though, parents seem to think little of shelling out fifty euro or so on costumes that Disney would think twice about budgeting for. Ever since I visited the dark side of Hallowe'en and took on the financier's role, I have waged an increasingly lonely battle against this kind of thing. I nobly insist, however humiliated they might feel, that my kids persist down the bin liner and strappy sandals road. Unfortunately, this involves a certain amount of imagination and hard work on my part, neither of which I'm particularly given to donating to the inflated Hallowe'en party.

Which brings us to the other current crisis in this Hallowe'en home. A month ago – around the time the first Christmas trees were going up – The Small Girl requested suggestions and assistance with her dressing-up plans. 'Dress up as a baby,' I volunteered without giving the matter any real thought. I had once passed myself off as an oversized baby on Hallowe'en and I recalled it as a sterling success. But I had been twenty-two and The Small Girl is seven and still half a baby herself. In fact, she devotes most of her time and her considerable energies to trying to look as little like a baby as possible. In spite of this, she liked the idea but opted to leave the details to me. At the time of writing, with the hours ticking away in their little heads, I have set aside a towel for her to wear as a nappy and nothing else. She is considering partial nudity and I am contemplating her hospitalisation for hypothermia and my imprisonment for child cruelty. Still, if the worst comes to the worst, there is always my wedding dress. And at least in this household, she'll get no argument from her sister.

THE IRISH PROBLEM

SMALL GIRL: 7 YEARS, 5 MONTHS
BOY: 5 YEARS, 4 MONTHS
YOUNGEST: 2 YEARS, 11 MONTHS

The kids have started to suspect that living in Dublin is not all it's cracked up to be – and they don't even know about the exorbitant property prices yet. Their disaffection is based – as was my own, at their age – on their ineligibility for all the best competitions in town. The chirpy presenters on Cartoon Network might deliver a truckload of toys to your door if you can answer their pie-easy questions correctly, but only if you live in the UK. Those heartlessly cast in the exclusion zone, meanwhile, mournfully watch other kids get lucky and dream of a world where something actually happens when you press the red button on your remote control.

My own miserable Irish Catholic childhood was equally ineligible, though my bitter, bitter envy was all directed at those lucky little bastards with Blue Peter badges. Back then, it seemed every child of note had the little blue ship on their lapel, while all we had were Pioneer pins and, for the stone mad, button badges invited all-comers to '*póg mo thóin*'. Frankly, we weren't in the same league. Years later, The English Husband admitted that even he had a Blue Peter badge. I might have left him on the spot if it hadn't turned out that it came to him through unofficial channels and he only ever wore it in an ironic way. I didn't – don't –

understand what that means. There is no irony about Blue Peter badges; only eight hundred years of oppression, inequality and heartbreak. And while I'm down there, what did the *Jackie* think it was playing at, religiously offering the writer of its letter of the week a (stg) £5 voucher for Boots and printing stories about teenagers going to discos? Over here, feasting on such crumbs, we had neither discos nor Boots nor the means to write in and point these sad facts out. And my kids are getting worked up over a truckload of toys?

Still, it's nice to be in on the birth of the next generation of the national inferiority complex. I had actually thought we might have grown out of this by now – and I certainly believed that their Anglo-Irish background would mean my own kids would be fabulously well-adjusted and excluded from the general envy, but if anything, they are even more screwed up than the full-blooded variety of Irish child. We lived there, see, and we chose to leave it. This has become such a regular topic of mealtime conversation in our house that I'm thinking of introducing TV dinners into the house, just to avoid the awkward questions. But why did we leave? But why did we think it was better here? And is it too late to go back?

They really don't mind that they wouldn't be able to go out and play and call for their friends in London – a state of affairs that seems to constitute our sole argument against the place. They could stay at home and listen to Busted knowing they might see them in the shops at any moment. For in their heads, that is what London is: a wondrous place of pop stars and interactive television and truckloads of toys rolling up to your door just because you knew that the Power Puff Girls live in Townsville. I remember believing much the same thing, and I didn't even know about the playgrounds. They, though, have been there and The Small Girl even remembers living there. She is quite the evangelist too, telling the others about all the fabulous playgrounds she frequented there and how there were five of them within walking distance. In fairness, she has a point. Back in Dullsville, we have to drive to our nearest playground. And although we've now been green-lighted for a new one a little closer to home, it's taken years of lobbying a council that originally decided our area was 'too well-off' for a playground. Go figure.

But for all her protestations, she knows which side her insecurities are hung up on. Driving through Liverpool last weekend, she spied a Union Jack flying a little half-heartedly from some official building or other. And quietly, entirely to herself, we heard her whisper, 'Boo England!'

Within hours, she was privy to an absolutely absurd argument between her mother and her paternal grandmother over who had killed the most people, the Germans or the Brits. This unseemly altercation took place underneath a rusty old German U-boat, raised to a position of pointing and staring at by the ship-yards of Birkenhead. Told it was German, The Small Girl had responded, 'I love the Germans; they're so clever.' 'Actually, they killed a lot of people,' corrected the woman who, in fairness, was almost amongst them, 'And they're not very nice at all.' Seconds later I was shouting about famines and colonialism and India while my unfortunate mother-in-law could do nothing but look on, open-mouthed. The Small Girl was delighted, though. Proud even. Sometimes I think we still have an awful long way to go. But frankly, a few decent prizes would make the journey so much easier.

CLOWNING AROUND

SMALL GIRL: 7 YEARS, 5 MONTHS
BOY: 5 YEARS, 4 MONTHS
YOUNGEST: 2 YEARS, 11 MONTHS

With fingers crossed, unfashionable Catholic aspirations on my lips and several types of solid wood within reach, I can safely say that happily, my kids enjoy rude health. It is just as well: were they ever to find themselves at its mercy, the latest development in the health service would do for them in an instant. Forget about big needles and nasty medicine; the latest menace to threaten our (well, my) children's mental stability is Clown Doctors.

Yet, according to my daily newspapers, they are on their way. Buoyed by the success of similar schemes in America, predictably enough, the white coats at children's hospitals here are to introduce medics masquerading as children's entertainers in an effort to keep little patients' spirits up. By all accounts, Robin Williams had a deal of success with just such a wheeze in the film *Patch Adams*, which certainly seems like reason enough to try it out in real life on really sick children. I can only hope they are made of sterner stuff than my own kids – the mere whiff of a clown can send them into paroxysms of fear. The idea that one might visit them while they're in bed would frankly probably kill them. So we are now living in fear of a fracture. We could (just) live with trolleys and waiting lists, but the dawn of the Clown Doctors is a different matter entirely and a far more daunting one.

I'm not sure how the Clown Problem started, though its first manifestation came some three years ago at the ringside of

Fossett's Circus. An unexpected upgrade had seen us move from the relative anonymity of the bleachers to front-row seats that were guaranteed to attract the attention of the clowning fraternity. In time, inevitably, they came for us – or rather, they came for The Boy, who at two-and-a-half, was just ripe for emotional scarring. Even as they cast their comedy butterfly net over his little big head, the clowns realised they'd made a terrible mistake. Simply, he went mad. I have seen him going mental many times since, but that afternoon remains the yardstick by which all his subsequent turns have been measured. I gather it may yet become the gold standard of nuttiness worldwide.

He faced the wrong way for the rest of the circus, sobbing throughout into his father's sodden shirt. Why didn't we take him out? Partly because we wanted to see the wild animals in cramped quarters, but also the whole upgrade thing and its associated spotlight made it all a bit awkward. So we gambled on our son's sanity for fear of appearing ungracious. In years to come, it will be for Anthony Clare to judge whether it was a winning ploy.

Anyway, as a direct result of all that, we nearly had to abandon a foreign holiday the following summer when he spotted Ronald McDonald at Dublin Airport. Cue further hysterics, emphatic refusal to go on plane, etc. Why didn't we just give into him? Oh, alright, we're bad parents and we really needed a tan.

He has had a pathological fear of clowns ever since and, probably because of her proximity to his paroxysms, The Small Girl shares his fears, albeit on a less spectacular scale. And now we have a full set – at Ikea in Warrington a couple of weeks ago (incidentally, the campaign to stop the hellish Ikea from coming to Dublin starts here), a gruff-voiced clown tried to cheer up the miserable Youngest by invading her personal space and smelling of stale beer. Surprisingly, it didn't work. In the glorious tradition of the family, she too went berserk. As we left, The Small Girls sadly conceded that 'we're not really good with clowns'. But at least we have our health.

But it can't just be us. Anyone who's read Stephen King's *It* must surely share our fear of clowns and anyone who's had to spend a day with them, as I did for a radio report a few years ago, must know that they're the least funny humans on the planet, and amongst its most miserable. And I'm totally with the little people on the Ronald McDonald thing – I sometimes think the multinational has been successful in spite of, rather than because of, its unsettling mascot.

But as long as they were contained in circuses, fast food outlets and horrible furniture warehouses, we could manage the Clown Thing. But now they are to be dispatched to the hospitals, those very places where, even in spite of everything that has(n't) happened, you expect succour and sanctuary, particularly for Small People. The news that there is now a real chance that a clown could cast a net over an injured Boy means that we won't be troubling the health service in the near future.

As if I didn't have enough to do, now I'm going to have to qualify as a doctor as well. Luckily, I've seen *Awakenings*, in which Robin Williams also plays a doctor, though in this instance, a non-comedic one. If I go through it frame by frame, by Christmas I should be better qualified than most of the doctors in casualty departments. And with the reassurance that our home is a Clown-Free zone, I'll probably get more sleep than they do as well. My God, I might even do house calls. Though I'll be charging extra for the jokes.

MORE (OR LESS) TEETH

SMALL GIRL: 7 YEARS, 6 MONTHS
BOY: 5 YEARS, 5 MONTHS
YOUNGEST: 2 YEARS, 11 MONTHS

The Boy might not yet know what he wants for Christmas, but according to all-comers this week, he might take his cue from a well-known song. Two years after its nearest neighbour was brutally knocked out in an accident that still has the capacity to ruin my appetite, his fragile front tooth has finally given up the ghost. My son is not yet five-and-a-half, and he has no front teeth. With the benefit of hindsight, I can't help thinking of all the money we might have saved on toothpaste if only we'd known.

It's not right, of course, but even I would have to concede that on the scale of wrongness, it ranks pretty low. Losing his first tooth when he crashed down onto a metal bar at the swimming pool remains the worst thing that ever happened him, and it ranks pretty close to being the greatest woe that ever befell me as well, and from that point of view, I hope it stays fine for us both. But it set us all on tenterhooks regarding the surviving front tooth, which wiggled and jiggled and briefly changed colour to the extent that the tooth fairy has been on permanent standby for two years. But miraculously, it hung on, until a couple of months ago, for no apparent reason, it suddenly started getting jiggy again. The dentist – by now a familiar figure in The Boy's young life – was consulted and an x-ray taken. Two years ago, we were warned that the angle of his fall might preclude him ever growing a permanent front tooth; two months ago, oh blessed relief, the miracle of radiation confirmed that there is not just one, but a pair of adult teeth on their way down. The sad, lonely baby tooth was wobbling, it turned out, simply because its usurper was in town.

But while the x-rays were greeted with unbridled euphoria by the parents – currently wondering what the hell to spend the SSIA on now – it's hard to reassure a Boy who isn't yet five-and-a-half and who vividly remembers the pain and the blood of his last tooth lost, that this next one is a positive development. And it certainly didn't help that in the end, it was a punch in the face from his younger sister that speeded up the process and severed all but the final thread by which it hung, precariously, for another couple of hours.

In an ideal world, after spending those hours lying on the sofa weeping – missing his favourite dinner in the process – The Boy's tooth would have dropped gracefully from his mouth to the applause of his supportive family, and his horror of losing his teeth would have been ended forever. Instead – because his life to date has been anything but charmed – here's what happened: after several hours of moaning, 'I won't let it happen, I won't', he fell asleep on his mother's lap and was carried up to bed, where, some hours later, the tooth left its moorings and he promptly swallowed it. The first we knew of it was a surprisingly angry summoning to his boudoir to confirm his worst fears. He spent the rest of the night puking his ring – but unfortunately not his tooth – up, his misery only briefly suspended when he found a shiny €2 coin under his pillow.

The following morning, over a hearty breakfast of spaghetti Bolognese and Coke, a happier, brighter, gummier Boy speculated that the tooth fairy might now acquire a tiny diving suit and head for the ocean bed to retrieve the tooth from the poo he had yet to do. And once the motion in question was behind him, life picked up again and already it is as though he never had teeth at all. The mad part of me, meanwhile, feels curiously deprived of three years of photogenic smiles, and if I might speak on behalf of the malodorous tooth fairy, robbed of the chance to collect a particular keepsake of early childhood. But in a world where bad things happen to good people, it's a tiny complaint and barely a regret.

It helps, of course, that he is a substantial boy. He hasn't looked not yet five-and-a-half since he was four and a bit, and so the gaping hole in his mouth looks more like an act of nature than a whole four acts of Shakespearean tragedy. And my, it's some hole. I can only assume the teeth-in-waiting are the size of tombstones and that the same nature that has been on sabbatical for so much of his young life has big plans for The Boy. When he sneaked into my bed for a cuddle the morning after the tragedy, I held him tight and for the first time, I felt definite biceps lining up under his pyjamas. And already, as he never tires of telling me, he is up to my diddies. It's not so long since he was sucking at them, now he's using them as a yardstick. He may not yet be five-and-a-half, but he is a man, my son.

CHRISTMAS COUNTDOWN

SMALL GIRL: 7 YEARS, 6 MONTHS
BOY: 5 YEARS, 5 MONTHS
YOUNGEST: 3 YEARS

If you aren't drowning in Christmas spirit by now, then frankly, you aren't doing it right. This is the time when humbug turns to hysteria, the manic, panicky, precious hours when even the coolest consumer hyperventilates at the sheer preposterousness of the amount of work to be done versus the time in which to do it. If you are mad like me, then these are the best hours of all. Even if you're stone cold sane, jump on board and enjoy the ride.

The tingly feeling has hit our home by degrees this year. The Boy has been vibrating gently since the middle of November, when he began drawing pictures of Santa with the kind of zeal that has seen older men arrested. In fact, if the unthinkable happened and Santa was ever murdered, I think it's safe to say The Boy has already drawn himself as the chief suspect. Our living room is currently a sort of shrine to Santa, his likeness – or at least, his vague resemblance – staring down from every conceivable angle. The idea behind the project is simple: no matter which way the Main Man happens to turn when he's about his business tonight, he is bound to clock a picture of himself and be suitably impressed. There are also quite a few drawings of Rudolph on the wall, though we've pointed out to him that Rudolph won't actually be coming into the house. So how come he eats the carrot left on the fireplace? The Small Girl wants to know. She's asking a lot of questions this year.

For my own part, the tingly feeling arrived in earnest about a fortnight ago. I never put up much of a fight, to be honest, but I didn't realise I was pulsating until I tried to describe the Guinness ad with the Christmas Eve snowfall to The Husband and burst into tears in the process. This happens to me from time to time and surprises nobody more than myself. The last recorded appearance of this advertising-induced sentimentality came when I tried to tell the sister who didn't have a television about the Jason McAteer Carlsberg ad during the last World Cup and ended up gasping great sobs of emotion instead. There was a similarly unsavoury incident involving the old ESB ad where the teenager comes home for

Christmas and his mother gets the house ready to the tune of 'I think I'm going back', but I think there may have been drink involved on that occasion so it probably doesn't count. I also cry every time I hear 'Fairy Tale of New York', so as you can imagine, December is a bit of a roller coaster for me.

But between crying jags, I never understand adults who say they hate Christmas. Unless something terrible has happened that is forever associated with the season, there is simply no excuse not to enjoy this time when a sense of international giddiness prevails. Even sober newspapers, in planning a Christmas Eve edition, concede that it should be full of good news and a general air of silliness. If you are looking for in-depth analysis on the future of Fallujah today, horseman pass on by (and get off that high horse, while you're at it).

I mean, what is there to dislike? The bonhomie, the good food, the generous measures, the presents, the charity, the candles, the glitter, the glamour, the parties, the fuss? The old friends, the family reunions, the chocolates, the excellent television? Surely even the most curmudgeonly cur can't hate the whole lot. Can a loathing of carols, alcohol and James Bond really exist in the same person? And what sort of unholy trinity would that make them?

Even if you can manage to muster opposition to all of the above, then I defy the hardest hearts to dismiss Santa as part of a package of humbug. Perhaps it is Santa who turns this cynic into a sap at this time of the year – and on this day in particular – but when there are three little people whose entire happiness currently depends on the Big Man delivering the goods in just a few hours, then it's hard not to be touched by his magic. It isn't just The Boy who's besotted: the whole family, even those who should know better, is on tenterhooks. Perhaps those who know better are mindful that in second class, some kids are already asking bigger questions than The Small Girl and it's just possible that by next year, the answers won't fit. And in the meantime, finally, The Youngest has managed to separate her birthday, a few days ago, from Christmas, and her traditional confusion has disappeared in a sea of red and white. Santa Claus – and maybe for one year only – has my kids totally in the palm of his white-gloved hand.

This evening, we will watch him leave the North Pole on the news and then it's quite possible that the excitement levels in this house will cause it to explode. Before it does, may I wish you the joy of Christmas and for those who can't feel the tingle, may you at least share the peace.

A NEW ARRIVAL

SMALL GIRL: 7 YEARS, 7 MONTHS
BOY: 5 YEARS, 6 MONTHS
YOUNGEST: 3 YEARS

Due to a typographical error in a painfully thick newspaper, I settled down over Christmas to watch something called 'The World's Strangest Man'. Before I realised the error of the sub-editor's ways, I must confess that I was wondering how many of the finalists I would know personally, while simultaneously quietly congratulating the producers on what sounded like a winning formula. Indeed, now that I know it was all a horrible mistake, I might even consider pitching it as a programme idea myself. Perhaps I could flog the whole concept to Ryan Tubridy, especially now that he's given up his gig on the 'World's Strangest Women'.

But back to the strongest men, for it is they. I can't be the only yuletider who's put in time with a mince pie in one hand and a bullet of a chocolate in the other, stuck in front of some Gunther or other with an alarming mullet and an ill-judged love of lycra. But why? What is it about truck-pullers and boulder-lifters that compels them to keep their powder dry all year and then splash it all over come Christmas time? Why has 'The World's Strongest Man' become a feature of the festive schedules, as much a part of Christmas now as crackers and cheesy greetings? And why do they always film it in brilliant sunshine in brilliant places? Who decided that people, hung-over and bound up on ruby wine and smoked salmon, would like to spend an hour watching an overweight German lifting a girder with his teeth in Florida? And could I interest them in 'The World's Strangest Man'?

As you might surmise, I managed to pack in an impressive amount of television over the past couple of weeks, largely because I was nursing our newest arrival. Yes, less than a month after I changed my last human nappy – having enjoyed just twenty odd days out of the last seven and a half years without contributing to Pampers' coffers – I changed my first Baby Annabel nappy. Frankly, I had hoped for a longer hiatus.

At least Annabel doesn't actually soil her nappies, as some other plastic wonders apparently do. But, oh, she makes up for it in other functions. 'She's so real,' the diminutive mother in the television ad promised, and so she is. Baby Annabel sucks, dozes, wakes up, breathes, laughs and cries. But mainly she cries. At least, she does now. For a week after her arrival in our lives, she was blissfully silent, largely because we decided not to put her batteries in. Her new mother, as it turned out, was perfectly contented to supply the sound effects herself and so we allowed her to role-play away with the relatively lifeless doll. But eventually – if only to sate my own curiosity – the batteries were inserted and Annabel came into her own. 'She's so real,' echoed the absolutely delighted Youngest, before dragging her charge off to calm her down. An hour later, she was more stressed than a three-year-old has a right to be and Baby Annabel still wouldn't let up. So I did what countless new grandmothers before me have done; I took over. With the strain of new motherhood lifted from her, The Youngest returned to her brand new world of Balamory villagers and I settled down to bottle feed and then wind a baby doll. And because I am nothing if not slightly mad, I didn't mind in the slightest.

I did mind, later on, when The Youngest, taking a second run at motherhood, dropped Annabel on her head and then walked away to see what other damage she could do. And I minded a bit when she wanted to take her out but wouldn't allow me to put her lovely little pink coat and hat on. And I wish she wouldn't lie her flat on her back in her comfort seat because she can't see the television from that position and I'm worried she's not being stimulated enough, particularly when her mother is a flibbertigibbet who loses interest in her hourly. Still, I'm impressed that she bothers with her at all – but while the older two changed their minds daily on their Santa demands, The Youngest settled on Baby Annabel back in October and never wavered from her plans. I'm sure there is a maternal instinct in there somewhere – it's just that at the moment, the town planner in her is slightly more dominant. At the rate she's going, it'll be a minor miracle if she gets through her working life without bothering a tribunal.

But in the middle of The Youngest's miniature expansion, Baby Annabel still receives regular visits and occasional feeds. And the ones she misses out on, I'm there to provide. I'm not sure Penelope Leach would recommend a doll as an effective way to silence a biological clock, but hey, don't knock it. The Youngest is delighted, I've stopped having 'what if' conversations with The

Husband while drunk and am no longer considering putting clothes on the rabbit. And Baby Annabel, between crying jags, seems happy enough. As long as I don't try to breastfeed her, I'll still be (just) on the right side of sanity.

CULTURE VULTURES

SMALL GIRL: 7 YEARS, 7 MONTHS
BOY: 5 YEARS, 6 MONTHS
YOUNGEST: 3 YEARS, 1 MONTH

New Year's Resolution Number 17: to stop letting DIY dominate our weekends and to bring the kids on interesting outings instead.

So we take them to the National Gallery. The next day, I tell two people that we've been and both of them respond by laughing their heads off and enquiring after the scale of the disaster. On the basis that even we hadn't harboured high hopes of the excursion, I decide not to take offence.

But oh, how wrong we all are. The news that we are to visit the gallery – which I'd expected to be greeted with an equal mix of horror and confusion – is gratefully received and we all pile into the car, off on the first of our weekly adventures. We are not going to Funderland. Already, this is a triumph of parenting.

And it just gets better. We did have some concerns when, en route to the main event, we decided to walk around Merrion Square and look at the art on the railings. 'Crap!' The Boy trumpeted at most of the labours of love. 'Boring!' his big sister echoed, while they both chorused on a few 'Scribbles!' while the guilty scribblers looked on, unimpressed. But they each found something they loved and we spent ages looking at big-eyed cats and small children's bottoms, before we took a swift detour into the park for a lecture about Oscar Wilde and a go in the playground, during which no blood was spilt – something of a first for our family.

Then across the road to the main attraction, which went like a dream. We'll give it half an hour, I advised The Husband, who has a degree. But an hour later they were begging to see more and so we did the whole shooting gallery. Inevitably, it wasn't without some incident – I suffered a predictable panic attack in that big, roomy room and had to inch along the wall to get out of there. And The Boy set an alarm off by touching the frame of the Picasso, setting in motion an impressive amount of scarpering and talking into walkie talkies. But he'd recognised the painting the second he entered the room, see, (The Husband having a degree), and he was so excited he just had to reach out.

But aside from the twin panics – interior and exterior – it all went swimmingly. Afterwards, we had Diet Coke in the café and we shared a huge biscuit and nobody spilt their drink or fell off their chair. Then they each chose two postcards – The Youngest just wanted one, a big-eyed cat – and off we went.

And when you're on a roll, you're on a roll. When we got home, the three of them threw themselves into rehearsing the pantomime they'd made up for its world premier in front of their parents and their auntie. After that triumph – a performance without petulance – we had our lovely roast dinner and they ate all their vegetables and then afterwards, they each performed a party piece. Finally, with half an hour to go before bed, they asked – I swear to God – to be allowed watch a bit of *Fantasia*. When they were finally dispatched, I commented to The Husband that if anyone had been trailing us for that one day, they might easily have mistaken us for a posh family.

Of course, the following morning, in the mad scramble of getting them back to school, a stalker would have been left with no illusions as to our provenance. Lots of high-pitched shouting about shoes, arguments over whether it was more important to play with Lego or put on a pair of trousers, and the predictable smattering of foul language marked the start of another term. The Youngest's waking words were 'I want to go to the pub', and in a way, we all knew how she felt. But it had been a perfect day, even if it was, as I'm increasingly convinced, all a dream.

The downside is that it's set a lofty precedent for the rest of our little excursions. Given that the remainder of the family were perfectly happy pursuing the DIY/DVD weekend diet, it has fallen to me to choose the destination and the agenda for all these happy events to come. While the future is bright – and in my enthusiastic mind encompasses all manner of sepia-toned pictures of Us At the Zoo, Us Up the Mountains, Us At the Beach (think *Picnic At Hanging Rock* but without the unpleasant consequences), the weeks to come present a more difficult prospect. Our recent wild weather suggests that we are now closer to Kansas than the Kremlin – and in the absence of a convenient yellow brick road to follow – I am charged with identifying indoor pursuits to keep the budding cultural life of the family fed and watered.

In the company of in-laws, we've already ticked off the Book of Kells – glass cases too high; the National Museum – 'too much stuff'; and Malahide Castle – 'there's a short-cut to the exit through this small door,' I seem to remember was the exact phrase the guide used. The kids think the cinema offers the ideal solution, but the lady's not for turning. I want us to stroll around in exotic locations, seeing how other peoples live, learning about the human condition. Oh God. Funderland, here we come.

DIRTY THOUGHTS

SMALL GIRL: 7 YEARS, 8 MONTHS
BOY: 5 YEARS, 7 MONTHS
YOUNGEST: 3 YEARS, 2 MONTHS

And now, a message from our sponsors: Your child's high chair could carry sixty-eight times more bacteria than your kitchen floor. I can't believe I got food poisoning from my own hands. I can't believe I gave my own son food poisoning. I can't believe anyone can't believe I can't believe it's not butter isn't butter, but I don't like to go on about it.

Is it any wonder the world has become enchanted with Howard Hughes all over again? Everywhere we turn, there are people with pixilated faces warning us that we're all facing a germy doom. In one ad, they've even pixilated the harbinger's hands. What's the point in that? Is he afraid one of his colleagues will recognise his filthy index finger and refrain from borrowing his card index? Do people still use card indexes?

The pixilated people almost ruined Christmas for me, and last summer they prevented us from having a barbecue at all, for fear of legal repercussions. Who times their food? Who knows when their marinated skewers have been ambient for forty minutes and when their turkey's been at room-temperature for an hour and who, in the middle of their Christmas dinner, is prepared to do anything about it? Does a high chair really have sixty-eight times as much bacteria as a kitchen floor? How the hell do they know how dirty my kitchen floor is?

If our slovenly ways in the catering department don't do for us, the latest message from the pixilated people is that the crap on our hands will get us. Literally. One of this year's Young Scientists did an unpleasant sounding survey and found that 33% of the handles on toilet doors in public places in his local area were infected with faecal matter. He lives in Clondalkin, by the way, in case you want to move. People of my own acquaintance are fond of warning all-comers against picking up peanuts from communal dishes on bars because most of them have traces of urine on them, and a charming nugget I read recently promises that if you flush the toilet with the seat up, you'll force faecal matter into the atmosphere at great speed. If your toothbrush happens to be in the same room as the toilet in question, the faecal matter can land on it and poison you. Since small children seem to be incapable of flushing with the seat down, this is heartening news for all the family.

Well, frankly, I'll take my chances. I wasn't born yesterday and in the days before pixilation, I'm quite sure I ate mountains of meat that had been ambient over the hour and, as the old people say, it's never done me a bit of harm. In fact, I'm well on my way to becoming one of those alarming grandmothers who stick their fingers in babies' mouths to calm them down while the new mother looks on from behind her sparkling steriliser, aghast. My own granny was an enthusiastic offender in this area: I remember presenting her with her first great grandchild, fresh out of neo-natal intensive care, and watching in horrified slow motion as she inserted a shaking digit into The Small Girl's tiny mouth. I won't delve into detail, but trust me, I know for a fact that finger had been in terrible places, not least the 1916 Rising.

But she was a woman who kept a coddle on the boil for most of her life without ever, ever washing the pot; a woman who believed a curious combination of soap and sugar could cure pretty much anything. And for the record, The Small Girl didn't hurl, just as her mother never hurled after eating hundreds of things off floors and high chairs. I also, in one particularly unfortunate incident, mistakenly ate some of The Small Girl's faecal matter without waiting for it to go through the plumbing first. And to the best of my knowledge, I haven't been particularly troubled in the intestinal department by my toothbrush either.

Is it just me? Have I a cast-iron constitution in a nation of soft shites? All those people on trolleys in A&E, are they really all there just because they didn't get the turkey into the fridge in time?

Might I suggest that the national campaign to make us all wipe our bottoms, wash our hands and for God's sake get me to the fridge on time, is merely symptomatic of the fact that we have little to worry about. We don't smoke anymore – although that intensely annoying woman on the ads could well drive us all back to it – most of us are off the drink for January and our SSIAs are all bubbling away nicely. But at a time of global crisis and disaster, it would be the height of bad taste for us to run a national ad campaign congratulating ourselves on the state we are in, to the tune of 'Happy Days Are Here Again'. So we've dug up some dirt.

When the big picture is rosy, you have to sweat the details. And when you're speeding towards secularisation at a rate of knots, then you'll find what you're looking for underneath your fingernails. Cleanliness next to Godliness, and all that. On the other hand, sometimes you just have to trust in God and eat the furry chocolate button you've found under the fridge. In spite of many claims to the contrary, I've found neither will let you down.

CEREMONIAL SHOPPING

SMALL GIRL: 7 YEARS, 8 MONTHS
BOY: 5 YEARS, 7 MONTHS
YOUNGEST: 3 YEARS, 2 MONTHS

It was the woman outside the playgroup who put the wind up me first. Not only had she bought the dress, she said, but she'd got the entire shooting gallery: the dress, the veil, the shoes, the socks, the slips, the knickers (they need new _knickers?_). And if I didn't sort myself out soon, she warned, there'd be nothing left. A quick straw poll of the veterans outside the school confirmed it – January and February are the months in which to do it, and if you haven't the whole lot organised by the end of February, your daughter will be the laughing stock of the parish. If you have a son, of course, feel free to do the shopping on the day before the Main Event, if you so wish. Nobody will be looking at him anyway – they'll all be too busy pointing and staring at the poor little girl whose slovenly mother thought it was okay to buy a First Communion dress in the same quarter of the year as the Communion.

So, as the Lord himself once said, it is accomplished. The Small Girl will go to the altar, and while I suspect there will be pumpkins there on the day – and possibly an occasional coach and four to boot – we will not be found wanting on the sartorial side. Now all we have to do is hang around for three months and pray she doesn't grow.

I must admit, I'd always regarded the First Communion shopping expedition as the single greatest perk of having a daughter. I further confess I'd even fantasised about the day that The Small

Girl and I would march around town, hand in hand, while the department stores and bijoux boutiques of Dublin happily surrendered to our every whim. Fleshing out the picture, there would be balmy weather (I had assumed we'd be a bit deeper into spring before the panic buying set in), a languid lunch break and profound conversation.

In the end, inevitably, the pressure of the whole occasion overcame us both. There wasn't a moment in the day when it wasn't raining, the lunch was a grabbed sandwich in a self-service restaurant – 'This is how they feed people in prison,' volunteered The Small Girl as we queued with our tray – and while openers like 'I love my brain' are certainly profound, they tend not to give rise to the kind of urbane exchanges I'd hoped for in the Woody Allen version of First Communion shopping.

But there were precious moments, nonetheless. The ready agreement, on the bus, that neither of us would have any truck with the frills and the frivolous; her explaining to me what 'buffy' means in terms of fashion design; her happy admission, after the first half-dozen tryings-on, that they all looked exactly the same to her and that she loved them all; her willingness to walk enormous distances in the rain in pursuit of the perfect dress; and then finding it, and the way she looked in the changing room and how all the other Communion shoppers looked at her and admired this tiny beauty in her simple, but buffy dress.

But still we couldn't buy it. What if she grew? What if there was one she (I) liked even better in one of those scary shops that most resemble an explosion in a cake factory?

So we carried on, even jumping a wheezing bus back out to the suburbs and a shop in which there appeared to be a small riot in progress. Here, the principal distraction of First Communion shopping – parent-watching – reached its peak. In Arnott's I'd been astonished to find so many fathers – traditionally passive and reluctant participants in this woman's world – actively driving the selection progress. Carrying armfuls of dresses, they travelled from clothes rails to changing rooms, like a snowy bucket chain, barking instructions at beleaguered eight-year-olds – turn this way, put that top on with that dress, try it with the veil – while the mothers seemed far more docile. 'Does that one make her look fat?' one father shouted at the rest of his family and several strangers as his princess poured into something shimmering. Another asked about underskirts. The next time the man in your life protests he knows nothing of shopping, don't believe it for a moment.

In the Beirut shop, they put the little girls on pedestals so everyone could get an eyeful. By the time we got there, there wasn't a pedestal to be had and so we hogged a rail, two drowned rats wading through a sea of satin. Still, The Small Girl's perpetual good humour didn't desert her as she stood shivering in her little vest while her anxious mother forced more unsuitable items upon her. On a pedestal nearby, a beautiful child who'd clearly been to the hairdressers for the occasion showed herself off in increasingly flashy dresses. As each went on and the assistant confirmed it was the best yet, the little girl leaned delicately over and kissed her admiring mother on the lips. While both The Small Girl and I secretly suspected this child to be a cow, part of me couldn't help reflecting that I was more likely, at the end of our exhausting, confusing day, to receive a kick in the head from my daughter than an ostentatious show of affection. When it comes to The Boy's turn, of course, he'll be wearing the face off me. But in the meantime, I'll settle for a simple dress and a perfectly perfect girl beaming with pleasure inside it. And you should see her, you really should.

BIG SCREEN, SMALL PEOPLE

SMALL GIRL: 7 YEARS, 8 MONTHS
BOY: 5 YEARS, 7 MONTHS
YOUNGEST: 3 YEARS, 2 MONTHS

I don't think I've ever seen The Husband as incandescent as he currently is over *The Magic Roundabout*. I'll concede that it's not the greatest film we've ever seen, but given that nobody spilt their drink over themselves, got sick or fell asleep, I'm regarding it as a triumph of sorts. But The Husband – still haunted by what they did to *Thunderbirds* – just can't see the popcorn-bucket-half-full argument on this occasion. He is, as we used to say back then, bulling.

His biggest beef, he says, is with the script. It's not great, in fairness, and the few knowing nods in the direction of Dylan the rabbit's recreational drug use can't quite make up for an absolute lack of Shrek-style gags – but it's *The Magic Roundabout*, for God's sake. I can't remember ever being unable to eat my tea for a mouthful of guffaws at Ermintrude's antics. In fact, if I were to be totally honest, I think 'The Magic Roundabout' was a tradition more honoured in the breach than the observance in our house. It was a short ordeal to be endured en route to something more satisfactory, like 'Crackerjack' or 'Rent-a-Ghost'. (For all that, the first long-playing record I ever acquired was a recording of Dougal and the Blue Cat, a much-loved and in time hopelessly scratched story of a dastardly cat with a Northern English accent who dallied with Dougal and lived to regret it. The dog responded to the taunting, much to our delight, by shouting 'Bluebag! Stinky poo!' at him. At a time when the Looney family's entire record collection consisted of The Mass of St Francis of Assisi and Dougal and the Blue Cat, it was a house favourite.)

While I am not walking the streets fuming over it, I admit I share a fraction of The Husband's indignation about all these old reliables given new suits of ill-fitting clothes. I blame the *fin-de-siècle* rush to drag all those hoary old espionage programmes – the 'Mission Impossibles', 'The Saints', 'The Avengers' – onto the big screen. In spite of as many misses as hits, the lazy fashion for plundering the past has inevitably extended to children's programmes. Tim Burton's brooding Batman showed that the big people could be brought along for the ride and *Scooby Doo* was distracting enough fare – and made the whole world realise what a terrible aberration Scrappy Doo was. Fuelled by this and taking note of a whole generation of thirtysomethings waxing endlessly about 'The Clangers' on radio shows, film-makers have been rummaging in the Useful Box for other nuggets.

I really wish they wouldn't. In a couple of months time, we will be visited by a twenty-first century Willie Wonka and already, I'm terrified at the prospect. We're big fans of Gene Wilder's classic interpretation of Roald Dahl's most intriguing creation, but we also go big on Johnny Depp round here, so we couldn't wait to gather round the computer, old-style, and warm our hands on the sneak preview trailers of the new *Charlie and the Chocolate Factory* that have been bouncing round the internet for a while. But oh, it's all wrong. Johnny plays Wonka like a bobbed Chitty Chitty Child Catcher – a character who, by an unhappy coincidence, is a regular and unwelcome nocturnal visitor in these parts. If The Husband needs a holiday after *The Magic Roundabout*, then we are likely to need family therapy after the Here's Johnny version of Wonka.

Like Westlife cover versions, the old adage holds true of

children's programming: if it ain't broke, for God's sake, leave it. Part of the charm of the original 'Magic Roundabout' was the fact that Dougal resembled the head of a sweeping brush in the charge of a drunk person. We quite liked the slightly off hurdy gurdy sound the roundabout made, and while I'm more forgiving than The Husband, I too was outraged by a film that happily spent several million pounds and couldn't spring a few extra quid for Zebedee to announce it was 'Time for Bed' at its conclusion. I know we're sweating the small stuff here, but this is our heritage, dammit.

And what on earth was wrong with the old Willie Wonka? What made Tim Burton hit the pause button and think, I can do that, only better? Will Gene Wilder ever recover? And what next – Bagpuss in outer space? Fingerbobs with no fingers? And was the snail really sexually attracted to the cow in the original? (Alright, alright.)

At the dinner table after *The Magic Roundabout*, we talked about what children's programmes we'd really like to see made into films. I nominated 'Paddington', but only if the adaptation of Michael Bond's hilarious books is a faithful one. With a couple of glasses of wine inside me, I even considered tackling it myself. The Husband couldn't – can't – get beyond the *Thunderbirds* debacle, and so he stuck with it, hoping somebody would have another crack at it and validate his otherwise worthless childhood. He also quite likes the idea of a big screen 'Rhubarb', though only if they retain the original theme music. As to the little people listening avidly to these words of the wise and the wine, The Boy nominated *The Magic Roundabout*, The Small Girl said *Barbie and The Nutcracker* and The Youngest suggested *Chocolate Ice Cream*. Which just goes to show that where children and the movies are concerned, you really can fool all the people all the time.

POWER OF DREAMS

SMALL GIRL: 7 YEARS, 9 MONTHS
BOY: 5 YEARS, 8 MONTHS
YOUNGEST: 3 YEARS, 3 MONTHS

I'm not sure what sweet dreams are made of, but right now in this house, we seem to have lost the recipe. The Boy – never a frequenter of the nocturnal pleasures of bouncy cornflower fields and marshmallow clouds at the best of times – has been suffering awful nightmares for weeks and his ghostly mother, unfortunately, has been laid low with sleep deprivation as a result.

Like so much else in the world these days, it's all the fault of smokers. If people didn't still smoke, then companies like Nicorette and Nicotinel would go out of business and the first month of the new year wouldn't be cluttered up with their annoying advertising. Leaving aside the incredibly irritating series of ads featuring that perpetually sullen woman who's kicked the habit and now feels obliged to share every moment of her mundane existence with the rest of us, the ad that has wreaked havoc around here is the one featuring the six-foot, grey-faced cigarette that tries to ambush quitters every time they draw fresh breath. 'The Smokes Man', that perfidious creature has come to be called and for the first few weeks of this year, he took to visiting my son on a nightly basis.

Most nights he'd show up around two-ish, and we knew he'd entered the building because of the terrified cries emanating from the back bedroom. It was some consolation for his wretched victim that the Smokes Man was always followed by a slightly befuddled mother, warm from sleep and ready to offer all the cuddles and comforting a boy can take – which in the case of this boy, is an impressive amount. So long after the Smokes Man had disappeared into the ether, I'd stay in The Boy's bed until I was sure he was asleep again and then I'd creep back to my own cold bed, afraid to warm up on The Husband for fear it'd wake him and give him ideas. Somehow, I never imagined that getting a decent night's sleep could involve so much politics.

Anyway, regardless of whether the Smokes Man had made an earlier appearance, you could absolutely set your watch by his arrival every morning at 6am. I get up shortly after that in any event, and most mornings, for The Boy, the curtain call of his demon signalled the end of any attempt at sleep. So we'd get up together, he to make something implausible out of Lego for two hours before the school frenzy began and I to try to get some work done in the relative calm before the storm. This work, inevitably, was disrupted by a stream of questions from the other end of the room, covering vitally important matters like whether or not I've ever seen a fairy's garden fence, why Wednesday comes after Tuesday and why John Lennon got shot.

But all that is behind us now. As January faded away, so too did the Smokes Man. As soon as he stopped frightening the life out of us in every ad break and leaping into view in every chemist shop window, he stopped visiting the hapless Boy. Of course, the week he stopped coming was the same week I finally sought professional advice on how to deal with his ominous presence. Once the boy was equipped to kick his head in (the professional approach, as it happens. Who knew?), he simply stopped coming. Cowardy custard.

But in a move reminiscent of all that 'I stepped out and I stepped in again' shenanigans at Lanigan's Ball, he was only gone when somebody else showed up. This is the Bad Man, and he has continued to wreak havoc in the poor Boy's head and bed. All the professional advice in the country can't seem to conquer this particular nightmare, and my own efforts to place the demon have come to nothing. He is a Bad Man; that's as much as any of us know.

The only consolation to be drawn from all these restless nights is that I too had a Bad Man who blighted my nights and I turned out to be happy as a sailor. My own bogeyman was a tall, gangly creature, half-man, half-clown, who spent his evenings pursuing me through a row of prefabricated classrooms until I eventually hid in a huge bunch of balloons which he would then burst one by one. He never got to the last one – I always woke up – and to this day, I've no idea who he was, where he came from or where he eventually disappeared to. But for about two years, he was such a frequent visitor that had I been giving out air miles, he might have spent his retirement circumnavigating the globe in first class.

But he eventually did go, and I'm banking on the Bad Man following suit one day soon, leaving nothing more than a faint shiver in his wake. If he doesn't, I shall just have to jump in there and kick his rotten head in myself. And while I'm down there, I'll present him with the bill for the anti-wrinkle cream that I'm currently trowelling on as a substitute for sleep. He thinks he gives good nightmare? Wait till he gets a load of me without my make-up on.

PRESENTING THE PAST

SMALL GIRL: 7 YEARS, 9 MONTHS
BOY: 5 YEARS, 8 MONTHS
YOUNGEST: 3 YEARS, 3 MONTHS

You know you're getting old when your stuff starts making it into museums. I remember feeling a little jaded when I saw a suit of Maeve Hillery's propped up for the purposes of pointing and jeering in Collins' Barracks a couple of years back. I don't mean to be indelicate, but shouldn't we at least wait until people have shuffled off before we turn their wardrobes into a national laughing stock? But my concern for the former First Lady's sensibilities was pitched firmly into the ha'penny place by our trip to the Science Museum in London last weekend. It was bad enough seeing my granny's Hoover on prominent display beside the very first vacuum cleaner and an accompanying illustration of Victorian housemaids up to their elbows in dust. But the absolute proof that I am of another era was just across the aisle. There, being generally ridiculed by a troop of boy scouts, was our old washing machine. It was a Rolls Royce twin tub, the explanatory note confirmed for the benefit of the youthful majority, and it required the put-upon housewife to transfer the heavy, soaking washload from one tub to the other – imagine! – where it would spin like it was going out of fashion.

Which, clearly, it was. Our own twin tub came to an unhappy end when my new blue trousers got tangled up in the spinning mechanism and both washing machine and trousers were taken away by some men in a van. I cried my heart out as they went – as much for the washing machine as the trousers, funnily enough. (Perhaps I had some childish precognition of the fact that I would spend most of my adult life loading and emptying a shinier, soupier model.)

But at least I've outlived the twin tub, which is something. The next exhibit brought no such consolation. There, in the same display case as some cooking utensils that once served Henry VIII – a formidable task – was our microwave oven. Not my granny's microwave (she never got beyond the coddle pot); not even the one that my parents lifted from its packaging all those years ago and the whole family marvelled at how quickly it could cook a sausage, until we tasted it. No, there, direct from the past, was the exact model of microwave oven that currently lives in our kitchen and cooks my porridge. It's hardly the Tara brooch, for God's sake.

The other familiar household object we saw in the Science Museum, funnily enough, was Joe Duffy. He and his brood of Young Scientists were on their way out as we were coming in. He didn't warn me that our trip through the aisles might be more like an episode of 'Crime File' (oh, who am I kidding – 'Garda Patrol') than 'Time Team', but maybe the Duffy family has a more modern microwave than we do.

We were never likely to spot too many of our belongings in the Tate Modern – though much of it does resemble a junk yard – but we still reckoned it was worth a visit, particularly given our recent triumph with the kids in the National Gallery. And parts of it were very good indeed. Water Lillies and a clutch of Cezannes and Matisses for me; another couple of Picassos for The Boy; The Small Girl played a gallery-organised game called Art Detective, from which she learnt that she is very bad at removing stickers from their backing paper, and The Youngest slept through the entire experience while a lower – lower, mind – respiratory tract infection weaved its way through her hot little body.

But oh, there was an awful lot of bollocks going on there as well. It is practically impossible to be married to somebody who's been to art college and hold fast on an 'all art is rubbish' stance – though God knows I tried. But while I've conceded a huge amount of ground where the art world is concerned and picked up a surprisingly satisfying appreciation of some of the finer things along the way, I absolutely refuse to accept that a plain blue square is a work of genius. Or, indeed, that a couple of shop dummies sweeping up millions of paper cut-outs deserves a whole room in one of the world's most esteemed galleries. The Husband begs to differ, of course, but then, as I pointed out to him on the walk back up the South Bank, he is simultaneously a snob and a sheep where art is concerned. The difference between us, put simply, is that I believe that if you can't hang it on the railings of Merrion Square, it isn't art. He would contend that nothing on the railings of Merrion Square is worthy of the term. And so a heated debate ensued – the kind of rattling row the South Bank was built for. If I hadn't been taking so many cheap shots, I'd have felt positively cosmopolitan. At the end of the walkway, a man in a foolish shirt approached us and asked if we were going to visit the Saatchi Gallery. The kids looked scared but it was never going to happen. Still, The Husband helped himself to a handful of concession passes 'for the next time' and glared at me accordingly.

The following morning, over breakfast, The Small Girl asked me why that blue square is in an art gallery. 'Ask your father,' I cheerfully replied between mouthfuls of some particularly good wholegrain toast. It's little things like this that make half-term holidays – and life in general – so sweet.

BUNNY BOYS

SMALL GIRL: 7 YEARS, 9 MONTHS
BOY 5: YEARS, 8 MONTHS
YOUNGEST: 3 YEARS, 3 MONTHS

We have just had both The Boy and the rabbit immunised. Measles, mumps, mixamatosis – bring them all on, we will laugh at their best.

Neither medical intervention was without repercussions. The Boy, being a soft lad, had requested that his mother be on hand for his boosters to catch him as he fell apart. But cometh the day, cometh the tummy bug and misseth the appointment. On his return to school the next day, he was effectively ambushed by a Big Nurse character who called him out of class without giving him a clue why, then told him his muscles were massive and stuck a needle into each of them while I was having a grand old time just a couple of hundred yards away. As it happened – and in spite of the safe money being on such a strategy resulting in his being hospitalised in a basket – The Boy was quite pleased to be singled out for individual torture. The massive muscles thing thrilled him to bits as well, and full of bravado and miniscule amounts of chemicals, it was a happy bunny I collected that day.

I wish I could say the same for the bunny. But there had been no admiring glances or rudimentary psychology applied in his case – just a firm pair of hands and a hypodermic syringe that all the apologetic noises in the world couldn't explain to him. Cases of rabbits giving humans filthy looks are not particularly well-documented, but if anyone's cataloguing, we've now clocked up two. The second was directed at The Husband, who had the misfortune of being the schmuck who brought the rabbit for the jabs, and who has been *persona non gratis* in the rabbit world since. A fortnight ago, Man and Beast were practically drinking buddies, while I was regarded with the suspicion appropriate for the person in charge of locking down time. Now, the rabbit is my new best friend and The Husband is in rabbit coventry.

Anyway, there are bigger issues out there concerning the rabbit at the moment, which brings me neatly to the first recorded dirty look of our fun bun. That came last summer, when he was a mere kitten. When we bought him, he'd been too young for the pet shop people to tell us his gender, so when he was about twelve weeks old, I'd set my mind to settling the matter for once and for all. As a former owner and trainer of a crack team of guinea pigs, I fancy I can find my way around small mammals' genitalia. So, on a glorious evening, I scooped up our new charge, laid him on his back, and manipulated him in a manner that would reveal anything there was to reveal. Rebecca Loos recently did something similar with a pig on reality TV, though she was paid handsomely for it. For me, it's always been more of a hobby.

Anyway, out it came and in the same second, the unfortunate rabbit, male, threw me an absolute filthy. Feeling simultaneously like a vivisectionist and a slut, I quickly set him off on his travels again, but it was weeks before we could look each other in the eye.

But while I still shiver at the thought of it, the rabbit is suddenly so over it that he could give lessons to Victim Support. His salvation has come in the shape of puberty and suddenly he couldn't give a monkey's who sees his mickey.

I knew we were heading for trouble when, like The Boy, he suddenly developed massive muscles and – unlike The Boy – an accompanying pep in his step. While he's always enjoyed digging the odd depression, a couple of months ago, he began burrowing for Ireland. Holes, it seemed, were very much on his mind.

Then on Christmas Day, he mounted Barney. It wasn't a proud moment for anyone – he clearly had no idea what he was thinking of, Barney didn't know what hit him, and the custodian of Barney, The Youngest, shrieked that the rabbit was 'breaking Barney'. Bewildered, he was dragged off and dispatched back to the garden without so much as a brussels sprout.

It wasn't long afterwards that he found himself a girlfriend. That she is The Boy's football is a little depressing for all concerned, but in his own way, the rabbit's happy. He now spends all his waking hours gently pushing the lady into a position where he can mount her without having her skid out from under him. Then he does what he has to do – and with an enthusiasm for repeat performance that indicates how his species earned its hard-lovin' reputation. After a particularly dicey day last week, his little adventures indoors have now had to be curtailed. In quick succession on a twenty-minute play date, he rode a balloon, Barney (hurrah!) and a cuddly panda that I'm now afraid to touch. When he started sniffing round my legs, I reckoned enough was enough. I picked him up, noting in the short and speedy journey to the back door that he has grown considerably and no longer feels any embarrassment whatsoever about who knows it. Still proud and packing, he headed for the girlfriend and started shouldering her into a compliant pose. The Small Girl's happy cry of 'Look at Coinín! He's going mad!' was the final straw. The jig is up where he is concerned and he has been booked in for a procedure. Somehow, I suspect that as rabbit filthy looks go, we ain't seen nothing yet.

FIRST CONFESSION

SMALL GIRL: 7 YEARS, 9 MONTHS
BOY: 5 YEARS, 8 MONTHS
YOUNGEST: 3 YEARS, 3 MONTHS

If there is any casting of stones to be done this week, let The Small Girl do it: she is without sin.

I don't remember my own First Confession being much of an event on the social calendar – to be honest, it stays in my memory mainly because the man who heard it is currently doing a stretch at the pleasure of the state, for the usual business. I gather he confessed in the end; I am just relieved that when I went into the dark confessional for the first time, it was all one-way traffic.

They don't have confession boxes for children any more, of course. They don't even have Confession – or at least they don't call it that anymore. I like to think my finger is at least in the vicinity of the pulse of the church, but I'd no idea we didn't use the C-word anymore. I must have missed the note.

Anyway, it's called Reconciliation now, and the first dose of it comes packaged in a whole service with mams and dads and occasional grandparents and everything. It's funny really, because when confession was so good for the soul that we couldn't get enough of it, our very first one was a non-event, shoe-horned into the school day between the *Buntús Cainte* and lunch. Now, only the very old and blameless go regularly and the First Reconciliation is a standing room only event. Maybe it's because everyone knows that there won't be many more reconciliations after the first one.

Which I think is kind of sad. I have long been convinced that the decline in confessions is directly linked to the rise in depression and even possibly suicide. For generations, Confession was our therapy – and while I certainly wouldn't claim that we were nationally the better for it, I'm sure lots of us individually really were. I can still remember that extraordinary feeling of lightness and clarity that always descended on me walking down from the church after Saturday morning confession; the knock-me-down-now sense of never having had it so good. It's a feeling of well-being I've never been able to match – and I've spent a weekend in Inchydoney!

But like most practising Catholics, I rarely trouble the confessional these days – though I'm always in the market for a general absolution (I might even be prepared to travel for one, if anyone can point me in the right direction).

I don't really know why Confession has fallen into such a decline, but I'm fairly sure I don't want to be the one to stop the rot. A lot of confessions seem to take place on the altar nowadays, with everyone watching, which I don't much fancy in case somebody times me. Equally, I've an aversion to the more anonymous box lest a decent confession be followed by the standard, 'Are you the one off the Gerry Ryan Show?' question. The last thing I need is a priest suggesting a few more sins I should have 'fessed up to before I go.

I was once told that it's a sin not to go to Confession between Ash Wednesday and Pentecost Sunday, which always struck me as mad. Surely if you're pursuing the kind of sin-free life you promise to try to live in the confessional, then you've no need to confess anything within a regimented time frame. If Jesus was here now, would it be a sin for him not to go to Confession this month?

If it is a sin, then at least I've got a couple of things to get off my chest, so I probably should go – especially as I've now got a young companion to take. We were actually on our way to the service the other night when The Small Girl realised that she would be expected to go again, and I can't say she was best pleased. Her examination of conscience seemed to be a particularly tortuous experience for her, not least because everything that she's ever done wrong in her young life has been, somehow, her brother's fault.

But she got through it and returned to her seat beaming, even gleaming. She told me the priest had asked her brother's age, which did make me wonder whether she'd blamed the entire thing on him, and she then ploughed through the fastest penance in the west. On the way out of the church she pointed out a boy in her class who she thinks is 'dreamy' and I asked her if she felt she'd like to be hit by a bus. She declined.

The priest conducting the service had suggested the pint-sized penitents might consider making their second confession during Holy Week, but some of them are concerned they won't be able to come up with the goods (or bads, as the case may be) in such a short time. The Small Girl has no such problems. On Mother's Day, at 6.50am, she engaged in a ferocious argument with The Boy outside our bedroom door as to whether or not they should wake me to enjoy the breakfast they'd just noisily deposited at the side of the bed. 'You fucking arse face!' was her constructive argument. 'You said a bad word,' replied the newly-sainted Boy. 'On Mother's Day.'

In retrospect, I should probably have got her a big bucket of stones and had her cast them all on the way home from the church. She might even have hit a bus. Which in a way, would have been good for both our souls.

ATOMIC ENERGY

SMALL GIRL: 7 YEARS 10 MONTHS
BOY: 5 YEARS 9 MONTHS
YOUNGEST: 3 YEARS 4 MONTHS

Every time I hear the title of U2's current album, it makes me think of The Youngest. 'How To Dismantle An Atomic Bomb' might have been constructed with Bono's late father in mind, but no matter how much diplomacy was required in his handling, he can't have been a patch on our three-year-old. I'm not sure whether I'm the bull in her china shop or she's the bull in mine, but either way, I at all times trip through her (crossed) wires like an eggshell walker wearing asbestos kid gloves.

A typical scenario plays like this: she asks for milk and I give it to her. She complains that she doesn't like the green cup and bursts into tears. I produce a yellow cup and pour the milk from the green one to the yellow one. She then wails that she needs different milk. I put the milk back into the green cup and pour fresh milk into the yellow one. She says she wants apple juice. I pour the milk back into the carton, rinse the yellow cup and put apple juice in it. By now in a heap, she says she hates the yellow cup and wants the green one. I wash the green cup and pour fresh apple juice into it. She says she wants milk. In the green cup. So I pour the apple juice back into the carton, rinse the green cup and pour fresh milk into it, which she drinks between renting sobs.

There is an alternative ending. In it, the mother refuses to bring the green cup back into play once it's been initially rejected. The Youngest responds by pushing over the yellow cup and then throwing herself on the floor where she lies, screaming, for anything up to half an hour. But frankly, we tried that ending out and found we didn't like it as much as the original one.

I'm not sure what The Book says about letting the youngest child get away with murder but then, to be honest, I stopped reading The Book a long time ago. Things just always seemed to turn out so well in it. Also, I seem to remember looking up the word "nutter" in the index when The Boy was a baby, and it wasn't there. Nut allergy, yes; nutter, no. What kind of a child-rearing manual is that?

In the absence of a credible guide in these trying times, we have by and large opted for the easy road. I realise the scene I describe above doesn't cover me in glory either as a parent or a caterer, but I'm not convinced that the hard-line approach will teach her anything about the world in the long run, other than that our kitchen floor needs sanding. I would like to think that by the time she reaches adulthood, she will no longer feel so passionately about the colour of her cups and these little crises will pass without whoever is doing the pouring having to break out in a sweat. Admittedly, I have a horror that on her wedding day, our gorgeous blonde will break a fingernail or snag her hem on her way up the aisle and the marriage will be called off, the bridegroom sent to a hateful place and church-floor cleaners given a day off after the tafetta-polishing brings up a hitherto unknown shine.

But this sort of fingers-crossed approach to parenting only works when there are no other children involved. When other little people get in the way, it can be bloody. Take last Saturday, when The Youngest charged in from the garden and swiped a Bratz doll who was playing a key role in a complex adventure, principally conducted in The Small Girl's head. Cue Small Girl loudly protesting that it was her doll and also her game, and

Youngest bawling that she wanted to play with it now and anyway, she had it first. Now, in many ways, the path of least resistance was to appeal to The Small Girl's innate goodness and ask that she surrender the doll on the basis that she is seven and, as such, partly reasonable. But she was also emphatically right, and there lay the rub. When indulging a bold child involves punishing another perfectly good one, it's hard to start producing endless multicoloured cups. Sometimes, when all around you are losing their heads – and in spite of having devoured the contents of The Book back when everything was gleaming – you just don't know what to do.

As it happened, the Bratz crisis was resolved by a smart piece of sleight of hand on the part of The Small Girl, who simply substituted the disputed doll for another, equally vacuous-looking one. The Youngest, through her fug, never noticed a thing and believed she'd won the battle. The war, though, is ongoing – largely marshalled by The Boy, whose role in his sister's turbulent threes is to make everything infinitely worse. Sometimes I wish they could all get along, but most of the time I just wish I didn't have to be the referee. And the GAA officials think they have it tough? At least sometimes they get medals. And they have a handbook with whole chapters on how to deal with nutters.

EVERYONE A WINNER

SMALL GIRL: 7 YEARS 10 MONTHS
BOY: 5 YEARS 9 MONTHS
YOUNGEST: 3 YEARS 4 MONTHS

What shall we do with the Community Games? Aidan Walsh once asked. As far as I can recall, he didn't offer any answers to that perplexer but he would have been well placed to do so, having made his first few shillings videotaping the finals on behalf of the organisation. He even had Joe Connolly, Mr Community Games himself, on the record, chewing the fat of the games which Aidan memorably described as 'running and jumping and throwing the bow and arrow.' If you've no idea what I'm talking about, you really, really missed out on an extraordinary time in Irish life.

The Community Games themselves sort of passed me by, as it happens. When I was growing up, they were things other, swifter-footed children did, reasons for day-trips to Santry and Mosney that we never went on. I gather it was more about the taking part than the winning, but frankly, finishing last in every-thing is no fun at all; so on the days of the Community Games heats in our area, the Looney family collectively washed its hair.

I don't know if they had a choir competition in the Community Games back then, but they do now, which is why The Small Girl and I climbed on a minibus at an unseemly hour last Saturday morning and headed for the Dublin finals. Lest that sound more impressive than it actually was, there were no heats. To be honest, there was barely a final, but we'll come to that in due course.

It's years and years since I was on a tour bus with a bunch of prepubescent girls but, like Led Zepellin, I was reassured to find that the song remains the same. And it is 'Everywhere we go, the people always ask us.' On the journey to Artane and back, we heard it about, oh, a million times. I almost became a primary school teacher. Until last Saturday, I had never really considered what a lucky escape I'd had.

The questions remain the same as well. As the bus left the car park, headed for adventure and hopes of glory, another mother who is a teacher primed me as to the three questions that always get asked on these occasions. They are: are we nearly there?;

when can we have our lunch?; and do we have to sit in the same seats on the way back? Sure enough, before we'd hit the open road, they'd all been rolled out. The answers, for the record, were 'no'; 'after you've sung' and 'yes'. Apparently, there's a whole module in St Pat's devoted to divining just those answers.

As it happened, though, the rule book was about to go out the window. We rolled up at Artane Community Centre with a last blast of 'the people always ask us, the people always ask us' and found there was nobody there to ask us anything. Admittedly, we were fifteen minutes early. Forty-five minutes later, in the absence of any other competitors or indeed, a judge, we conceded that the lunches could be opened. It was 10.30am.

The Community Games official had, at least, shown up – and in an impressive official blazer. Having been already warned that the proceedings would take four hours, she revised the time downwards on the basis that there would be only one other choir competing. This was a bit of a shock, but did mean that our scrubbed-up charges would be guaranteed silver medals and – given that there was no sign of the opposition – was starting to smell like a team walkover. But an hour late, the other choir finally filed in. 'These always win it,' the Community Games official cheerfully reassured us. The judges, who'd arrived in the meantime, didn't demur. When they stood up half an hour later to give their verdict, the first thing they did was congratulate the other team for having shown up at all. And not in the kind of tone that, say, I might have used.

I've just read that last paragraph back and the flavour of sour grapes has overwhelmed even me. The thing was, our lot worked really, really hard and did really, really well and on the morning, they just didn't really get the credit for anything – including coming from the other side of the city and showing up on time.

Now I just sound pathetic. So I'll add that one of their spectators opened a packet of crisps and started eating just as ours piped up and then draw a line under the whole affair.

Which, for the record, Swords West were worthy winners of. And our cherubs were gracious runners-up and for some, stoicism didn't even make an appearance. As I watched The Small Girl beaming with pride as the silver medal was placed round her neck, I realised she thought they'd won. Twenty-four hours previously there'd been a huge kerfuffle when her birth cert had disappeared from the bunch, threatening her very participation. The Community Games, see, needed proof she was under sixteen. When we got home, several lunches and a couple more million renditions of 'Everywhere We Go' later, she changed into her age 4-5 shorts and disappeared off to show the world her medal. Winner alright.

So what should we do with the Community Games? Keep them going, Joe, because for thousands of sporty kids, they're a hugely rewarding experience. And for those whose talents lie more in the half-time entertainments line, a bit more encouragement could mean a whole lot of kids who never normally trouble the medals table will make the trip to Mosney. And hey, don't sweat the birth certs thing so much.

BEAUTIFUL DAY

SMALL GIRL: 7 YEARS 11 MONTHS
BOY: 5 YEARS 10 MONTHS
YOUNGEST: 3 YEARS 5 MONTHS

The worst part of my First Communion was a certain nun who pitched up a couple of weeks ahead of the Big Day and told us the story of Blessed Imelda. Imelda was a saintly child who loved Jesus so much that in the seconds before she received her First Communion, she was so overcome with religious fervour that, as the nun put it, 'her heart exploded and she died'. We should all aspire to be like Imelda on our special day, she advised us before disappearing in a flurry of black, leaving forty-five shell-shocked seven-year-olds in her wake. I can still remember sitting in the front row of the Holy Spirit Church in Greenhills on the day of days, my little heart pounding in my chest, and repeating over and over in my head, 'Please God don't let me love you too much.'

I had thought the spectre of Blessed Imelda had passed from my life until last Saturday morning in a different church when again my bigger, older heart started pounding with excitement and the awful prospect of loving too much. The vision sitting beside me – blissfully unaware of the cautionary tale of Blessed Imelda – was managing to calm her own jitters with an under-her-breath rendition of 'Beauty School Drop Out', which wasn't one of the songs we'd practised so painstakingly for the occasion, but hey, it worked for her. I, meanwhile, partly mortified by the discovery that I was more breathless about my daughter's Communion than I'd been about my own, sent out for water and resolved to try my best to remain conscious for the Mass ahead.

In any event, fainting fits weren't on any of my rosters. I had rosters. The one for Saturday was stuck to the fridge so that everyone affected by it could memorise it and answer questions on it should I have decided to perform some spot tests – though since such oral examinations weren't actually on the roster, they were just never going to happen. The reasons for the rosters were complex, but I'd heard too many stories of unseemly fighting over hot water and people (men) deciding to take the newspaper into the bathroom with them for a Saturday morning ponder on the Big Day to leave anything to chance. We had seven people to clean and present that day – the five of us, the godfather and the increasingly bewildered mother-in-law – and I was damned if anyone was going to spend longer than their allocated twenty-five minutes in the process. Normally I think I'm Lynette in 'Desperate Housewives'; last week, I was Bree.

Afterwards, somebody asked me how long I'd been planning the whole event and I answered that it was pretty much since I'd heard the words 'it's a girl'. But she wasn't just any girl, see. She was The Small Girl, a three-and-a-half-pound wonder who spent the first weeks of her life lying on a heated mattress in intensive care when she should have been in her terrified mother's arms, who fought like a tiny tiger to catch up with all the bigger small girls and who starts every day with a song in her heart and a dream in her head. Sometimes I tell her that she is my hero and one day I must tell her that I mean that more than she can ever know.

And on the day, she was just perfect. To be fair, they all were, even the boys, who I always feel a little bit sorry for on First Communion days. The mammies – who, frankly, wouldn't be troubling the Miss World people too much on any given Saturday – all scrubbed up beautifully (Jesus! One of us even got hair extensions!) and the weather, which the forecasters had warned would be biblical, managed to defy all predictions and resolutely failed to put a dampener on the proceedings.

After the Mass, it's all a bit of a blur (and not because of the indecent amounts of alcohol on offer). Restaurant, house, bouncy castle, friends, neighbours, food – way too much food – fighting kids, pissed-off rabbit, mad mother-in-law, hilarious 'bringing the wrong child home' incident, which on any other occasion wouldn't have really been funny at all.

At the end of the day, I asked the communicant if it had been the best day of her life and she told me that two things had prevented it taking the title. One, in the restaurant, she'd dropped her fork on the square inch of her dress that wasn't covered by a towel and had got a stain on it, and two, some of the bigger kids had knocked her around a bit on the bouncy castle. That night, after everyone had gone home, I put the dress in the washing machine and the following morning I sent her out in her pyjamas to bounce alone until it was time to put on her perfect dress again.

We had hoped to do a spot of family promenading on the Sunday but the weather really was too bad so I spent eleven and a half hours cleaning the kitchen instead. The following morning, I broke the habit of a lifetime and decided not to go to the gym but to stay at home and – hey! – clean some more. It was the first time I've been in the house on my own for longer than a few minutes since, well, since I heard the words 'it's a girl'. I celebrated by reading the paper, uninterrupted. I even briefly considered reading it in the living room. But that amount of excitement might just have made my heart explode.

AFTERWORD

I wrote the first of these columns eight years ago as a new and totally bewildered mother. The most recent, I wrote as an older, more experienced and still totally bewildered mother. If I have learnt anything from eight years of parenthood, it is this:

1. Breastfeeding is the best way imaginable of losing weight.
2. Buying children's shoes is only moderately more pleasant than giving birth.
3. It is possible to derive absurd pride from the most mundane situations – a single drop of urine in a potty; a T-shirt that isn't on inside out. It is equally possible to experience epic disappointment from a child who won't share their toys or from one who wakes too early on a Saturday morning. And where rejected home-cooked food is concerned, it is acceptable to harbour murderous thoughts.
4. Never serve spaghetti Bolognese to a child who is wearing white.

Above all, I have discovered that extraordinary phenomenon of time warping that is attached to parenting. The first year of The Small Girl's life seemed to last for five years in my mind and we have a million photos of her to prove it. The Boy's first years skipped along busily enough and we have enough pictures to half-fill a slim album. I might have a picture of The Toddler lying around somewhere if I look hard enough.

It was ever thus, of course. My own parents once forgot to take me – their third child – on a family holiday and there is no photographic record whatsoever of my Confirmation Day. I think that by then, they had simply given up. I can't really blame them. I understand from older, even more bewildered parents, that the whole time-flying thing goes into overdrive as the teenage years beckon. By then, I'm told, The Girls will walk around in a state of perpetual mortification over the general state of their parents and The Boy will have given up talking to us altogether. Peace at last. I'd say I'm looking forward to it, but I don't want to tempt the clock onwards. For the past eight years I've been desperately hanging on to every precious, wonderful moment and I intend to keep on clinging.

As Gloria and the Mississippi once memorably sang, 'One Day At A Time, Sweet Jesus'.

Fiona Looney
August 2005